A TOUCH
of the
SACRED

A TOUCH
of the
SACRED

A Theologian's
Informal Guide
to Jewish Belief

Dr. Eugene B. Borowitz &
Frances W. Schwartz

For People of All Faiths, All Backgrounds

JEWISH LIGHTS Publishing

Woodstock, Vermont

A Touch of the Sacred:
A Theologian's Informal Guide to Jewish Belief

2010 Quality Paperback Edition, First Printing
2007 Hardcover Edition, First Printing
© 2007 by Eugene B. Borowitz and Frances W. Schwartz

Library of Congress Cataloging-in-Publication Data
Borowitz, Eugene B.
A touch of the sacred : a theologian's informal guide to Jewish belief /
Eugene B. Borowitz & Frances W. Schwartz.
p. cm
Includes bibliographical references and index.
ISBN-13: 978-1-58023-337-8 (hardcover : alk. paper)
ISBN-10: 1-58023-337-6 (hardcover : alk. paper)
1. Jewish way of life. 2. Spiritual life—Judaism. 3. God (Judaism) 4.
Judaism—Doctrines. 5. Judaism—United States. 6. Reform Judaism. I.
Schwartz, Frances Weinman. II. Title.
BM723.B64 2007
296.7—dc22

2007036767

ISBN-13: 978-1-58023-416-0 (quality pbk. : alk. paper)
ISBN-10: 1-58023-416-X (quality pbk. : alk. paper)

10 9 8 7 6 5 4 3 2 1

Cover design: Jenny Buono

Manufactured in the United States of America

For People of All Faiths, All Backgrounds
Published by Jewish Lights Publishing
A Division of LongHill Partners, Inc.
Sunset Farm Offices, Route 4, P.O. Box 237
Woodstock, VT 05091
Tel: (802) 457-4000   Fax: (802) 457-4004
www.jewishlights.com

CONTENTS

Acknowledgments xi

Introduction. xiii

Part I. Seeking the Sacred One

1. We Can't Talk about God but We Must. 3

2. Where Is God? Answering a Nine-Year-Old 7

3. God and Mystery 11

4. The Many Meanings of "God Is One" 15

5. Is Our God Experience Authentic?. 18

6. The Jewish Idea(s) of God 21

7. Relating to God: Substance or Style?. 25

8. Accepting the World God Willed. 29

Part II. Doing Holy Deeds

9. Being Close to God. 35

10. The Act and Art of Praying 39

11. Moses' Prayer for Healing—and Ours. 43

12. How Shall We Comfort the Mourner? 47

13. Traditional Words of Condolence. 50

14. A New Phase in Jewish Piety 53

15. The Power of Creating New Religious Customs 57

16. Fanaticism and Zeal. 61

17. Who Is a *Mentsh?*. 65

Part III. Creating Sacred Community

18. A Mystical Model for Leaders. 71

19. How an Agnostic Community Came to Seek Spirituality . 74

20. The Appeal of Transdenominational Judaism 79

21. A Conflict over Interfaith Dialogue 83

22. How Liberal and Orthodox Jews Can Coexist 88

23. The Special Risk of Liberalizing Judaism 91

24. Catholic-Jewish Dialogue: An Autobiographical Note . . . 95

25. The Historical Case for Interfaith Dialogue. 99

26. Building a Community of "God-Fearers" 103

Part IV. Reading Sacred Texts

27. Letting the Psalms Speak to You. 109

28. Reliving the Sinai Experience Each Year 114

29. "Weighing" the Texts That Instruct Us 118

30. Putting Texts in Context. 122

31. Religious Authority in Judaism. 126

32. Integrating Jewish Law and Jewish Ethics 131

33. Jewish Decision Making 135

34. Innovation in Judaism: Yesterday and Today 139

Part V. Thinking about Holiness

35. Why Do We Need Theology? 147

36. Theology as an Afterthought 151

37. Why Historical Theology Won't Do 154

38. Jewish God-Talk's Four Criteria 158

39. The Brain-Heart Interplay in Faith 161

40. Four Ways to Understand "God Says ..." 165

41. Clarifying Some Feminist Ideas. 168

42. Jewish Beliefs about Evil 172

43. The Messianic Hope Today. 176

44. Life after Death 180

Part VI. Learning from Holy Thinkers

45. Why I Am a Theologian Rather than a Philosopher. . . . 187

46. Seven People Who Shaped Modern Jewish Thought . . . 191

47. Rationalist Thinkers and What They Can Teach Us . . . 196

48. Two Misunderstood Messages of Martin Buber 200

49. Mordecai Kaplan: Ethnicity in Modern Judaism 204

50. The Greatest Contemporary Orthodox Jewish
    Philosopher 208

51. The Ethics "Mystery" and Abraham Joshua Heschel. . . . 213

52. Covenant Theology: An Autobiographical Note. 218

Glossary. 222

Bibliography of Titles Mentioned in This Book 228

ACKNOWLEDGMENTS

W e are grateful to the individuals and adult education groups who encouraged us while critiquing our early efforts. Our project editor, Lauren Seidman, showed noteworthy tact and graciousness in suggesting many essential changes, and we honor her for that. Kudos also to Emily Wichland, vice president of Editorial and Production at Jewish Lights, for her invaluable help every step of the way, and to Bryna Fischer, our eagle-eyed copy editor. We are particularly indebted to Stuart M. Matlins, publisher of Jewish Lights, for his sage advice about how to speak to the heart of today's readers by respecting their sincerity as well as their minds. May many more blessings descend on his God-serving enterprise.

We know we could not have done this—as so much else—without God's help and we therefore say:

> For the wonders God has done for people,
> Let them thank God for God's steadfast love.
>
> *Yodu l'adonai chasdo*
> *V'nifl'otoav livne adam.*

Psalm 107:15

INTRODUCTION

So much of this book is personal that we thought we'd say a few words about why it is different from what you might expect. Yes, *A Touch of the Sacred* is another book about Judaism, but this one, like Jewish life itself, is full of variety. There are many fine books on Jewish history or holidays or belief or ethics (we know, we wrote one). This book talks about the many moods, deeds, and concerns that make up a caring Jewish life, with special emphasis on the kind of living that leads to believing. We have tried to reach for Jewish breadth—check the contents to see if we're exaggerating—by limiting each essay to a thousand words, with a few exceptions. Lengthier treatments abound, including a few of ours. One advantage to this literary asceticism is that the concerns of the heart, when strong, do not need many words—and this book comes from two Jewish hearts.

Too often, books on religion are written either primarily for the head or for the heart—as if thinking people don't also feel intuitively, and spiritual types never think much at all. Bosh! Here is our special mix for you. The pieces started with Gene, and Francie shaped and nurtured them. It is our hope that these pieces will serve as unique windows into Judaism—in bite-size, sacred "touches."

Please note that we use the term "liberal" as in "liberal Jews" or "liberal Judaism" in a transdenominational sense to refer to the great number of non-Orthodox, believing Jews.

A final comment: You don't have to read this book in any particular order. It wasn't written with one in mind. We've arranged these "touches of the sacred" into six general categories, not because they mimic the Mishnah's (the first standardized compilation of rabbinic teaching) structure but to make it easier for you to further investigate an area you particularly care about. Unfamiliar—and some better-known—terms are listed in the Glossary at the end of the book. Deviations from the Jewish Publication Society's new translation of the Bible are Gene's responsibility.

I
Seeking the
Sacred One

1

We Can't Talk about God but We Must

What follows is a bit of what I call theological therapy, the clearing up of some intellectual snarls that unnecessarily frustrate people when they read thoughtful books about Jewish belief. My specific concern here is acknowledging and justifying the paradox at the core of talking about God, which in turn may help you talk about God and also listen openly to others.

In a way, the difficulty is quite easy to understand. Normally, when we come across a strange object, we try to think of something reasonably like it; once you see a horse, it's a small mental jump to then recognize a giraffe or even a hippopotamus. Somehow we know to compare the odd creature with the known one. But that won't work with God because we insist God is one, which means among other things to be unique, that is, incomparable. We can't really compare God to any other "thing," and that means thinking about God will always have limits and will always involve uncertainty.

Early in Israel's history, the author of the Song of the Sea (Exodus 15) tried to praise God properly: "Who is like You among the [polytheistic] gods, *Adonai*?" (*Mi chamocha ba-elim, Adonai?*) The answer is so obvious that the poet never bothers, and Jews have been singing the Mi Chamocha as part of our prayers for as long as

3

anyone remembers. If, however, we insist on an answer, the author of Psalm 86 offers it unambiguously in verse 8, which is often chanted as part of the liturgy for reading the Torah: "None of the [so-called] gods is like You, Adonai [my Lord]" (En kamochah ba-elohim, Adonai). (Although Adonai literally means "my Lord," it is used here and elsewhere in this book as a euphemism for God's Personal Name, YHVH, which is never pronounced.)

While that certainly is great praise, it does admit to a kind of ignorance on our part. If you can't compare God to anything, then you really can't say much positive about God, except that God is different from everything else.

We can put our problem with knowing God this way: We'd really have to be as great and as smart and as wise as God in order to gain a reasonably accurate understanding of Who or What God is. Our predicament is given memorable form by the great twentieth-century Jewish philosopher and theologian Abraham Joshua Heschel, who said: "Every statement about God is an understatement."

The Rabbis of the Talmud—the Jewish compendium of law, wisdom, and folklore—dealt with this conundrum by instructively misreading Psalm 65:2. Its literal translation is "Praise befits You." The Rabbis midrashically—that is, by imaginative interpretation—understood the Hebrew to say "For You [Adonai], silence is [the only fitting] praise." In other words, what might a person say that would ever be adequate to God's reality? Isn't that why the soundless, wordless prayer-moments at the end of the Amidah, the standing, eighteen-benediction prayer, are many people's favorite part of services?

But for all our appreciation of the limits of language, it just isn't human nature to remain silent in the face of utter greatness. Here are some instructive comparisons for our refusal to stay dumb. We may bumble, but we still think it useful to try to say audibly why we find this painting or sculpture exquisite, or this wine exceptional. Note the prefix "ex," which hints at something that stands out.

And God help the passionate lover who, even stammeringly, doesn't try to find language to say how much he or she cares. We spend so much of our lives trying to find words that "ex"pose who we truly are and what we truly feel, it's no wonder Aristotle called us the "speaking animals."

More than a thousand years after Aristotle, the kabbalists, medieval mystic Jewish teachers, resolved this paradox ingeniously. They said that God is ultimately the Limitless One, *En Sof*, of Whom, therefore, nothing at all might properly be said, not even this. But simultaneously, the kabbalists also insisted that God could be known in marvelous detail through ten spheres or nodes, *s'firot*, arranged in a significant configuration, that name the divine energies. The many permutations of these divine attributes, multiplied by the great variety of biblical metaphors describing God, gave these late-medieval mystics an apparently inexhaustible number of ways to depict aspects of God. Just how the God of Whom nothing might be said is indivisibly one with the *s'firotic* God of Whom almost anything might be said is the great religious mystery at the heart of Kabbalah.

The bulk of the Jewish community, however, found this solution to the God-talk paradox utterly beyond them. Instead, they used two strategies for responding to the can't-talk–must-talk dilemma. The intellectual minority who wanted to think about God with philosophical clarity declared what could and couldn't be said about God and then tried to stick to the rules they had created.

The more common way of dealing with God's inexpressibility has been to take for granted this sage maxim: Jewish statements about God are *never* literal; they are *always* figurative. This is easier to remember when we are reading poetry. We know that God isn't really our Shepherd or our King. Yet these and other metaphors can offer significant insights into special aspects of *Adonai*.

When we read prose, we often forget that God only figuratively may be said to "say," "hear," "smell" or "get angry." Even as unanthropomorphic a term as "one" would be improperly used to describe our God, if we took "one" in its sense of the beginning of a series, as in 1, 2, 3, 4.... Our God isn't merely the first of many other gods. Nonetheless, such allusive language, while not literally accurate, is neither empty of significant content nor devoid of truth. It assists us to presume a good chunk of Who or What God really is. Metaphoric language is a wondrous human accomplishment.

One final comment: The reason music, body language, silence, and the like play such important roles in religious life is that they communicate what lies beyond even our best words. Hyperbole, extreme exaggeration, is another way of reaching beyond ourselves. Allow me to use hyperbole to help you keep this theological therapeutic session in mind. Try imagining all the religious prose you read as lyrics awaiting the music of your soul to give them flight. On occasion, all of us can soar!

Where Is God? Answering a Nine-Year-Old

2

I have all sorts of poor reasons for apologizing before I say what I want to say. Yona is not likely to have long kept in mind the questions she asked her mother just before going to sleep one recent night. Even though I got an e-mail from Yona's mother the very next day, asking for help with her child, the theologian, I rationalized that it was already too late to talk about last night's hot topic. The minds of most children would have already gone to other matters. Besides, the questions were difficult! I told myself that her mother had done the most important thing she ought to have done in such a situation, particularly when one is as intellectually able as she. She responded as best she could in a thoughtful, loving, and brief way. I stress the last because to this day my family hesitates before asking me a question, for fear that my love of explaining things will bring on a long lecture.

In any case, being fearfully busy, I never answered the e-mail. Instead, I rather quickly spoke to Yona's mother to offer excuses for my failure to respond in kind. Since that time this matter has troubled me, particularly because Yona is admirable, as you will soon see from her questions. Though I now intend to atone for my sin, I have considerable qualms about how I may have mishandled all this.

Here are Yona's questions, as best as her mother could remember them:

1. Mom, I don't really get what God is. I know God is not a person. Should I call God "It" then?
2. I don't understand how it is that God is in everything. Say God is in a tree and you cut down the tree. Does that mean you are cutting down God?
3. If God is in this house and we are tearing down this house [Note from Yona's mother: "We're moving to a new house and this one indeed is being torn down."], where does God go?
4. If God is together with me and you, and then we each go in different directions, where does God go? [Also from Mother's note: "I did my best to try to speak with her about God ... but she continues to be befuddled."]

The most truthful answer I could give to Yona and her mother is, "Me too." The only advantage I have is that as the great Swiss psychologist Jean Piaget taught years ago, Yona is still a concrete thinker, while I, in my mature moments, have gone on to think abstractly. While that helps me avoid having too small a sense of God, it doesn't mean that I can now fully understand God. Despite the greatest abstractions I can think up, I have to admit that I and everyone else who has tried to think hard about God only end up even more befuddled. Having made these few observations—and fairly concisely, I may add—I believe that Yona's questions deserve a more direct response.

Since Yona attends a Jewish day school, her first question, about addressing God impersonally as "It," might best be concretely answered by using Hebrew terms she may know. The Rabbis of the Talmud certainly do something like that. They call God by terms that we don't find in the Bible. A number of them are impersonal, like The Power, *HaGevurah*, or Creator of the Universe, *Borei Olam*.

I suppose I should leave it at that but—here I go—I feel I have to add a little more explanation (though hardly a lecture!). That's why many Jews like the term The Name, *HaShem*. It's not what you'd call a person, but I guess only persons have names. So some thinkers today prefer to imagine God as a Power or Process, something like gravity or light. But most Jews prefer to combine the two ideas—God not being a person and God being something like a person. That way, neither one wins out. A favorite Jewish way of talking about God is *HaKadosh*, The Holy One, which does sound like an "It," but not if we quickly add *Baruch Hu*, blessed be He, which sounds like a male person. Or you could use a term that can simply means God's Presence, Shechinah; its feminine ending lets you know that God is being spoken of in "the female," as it were.

Yona's second question, about God being in everything, is another good example of concrete thinking. God is like the air in a balloon or the juice in an orange. Our Rabbis thought that God was even greater, and they invented a wonderful way of saying it: They called God "The Place," *HaMakom*. Everything has to have a place. You can move something all you want; it still has to have a place. No matter what you do to any single thing, it still has a place. The Rabbis put it nicely, "God is the place of the universe." Since this is hard to understand, they then added, to make sure they hadn't squeezed God into just our world, "But the world is not God's [only] place" (Genesis Rabbah 68:9).

When we start talking about things in Judaism that are this complicated, we often think it's better to try to say them as a poem than as plain language. That's why many Jews and other people who use the Hebrew Bible love the Book of Psalms, *Sefer T'hillim*. Things we can't figure out in plain language somehow reach deep down in us when they appear in a poem. In Psalm 139, the poet talks about what a remarkable mystery God is, because God is everywhere you can ever go. And if that were not enough to confuse anybody, the poet talks about how amazing it is that a person gets made inside the mother, and then grows and learns how to live on her or his own (Psalm 139:6–14).

If it would be possible to understand what the Rabbis meant about God as The Place of the world, then Yona's last two questions would pretty much answer themselves. We could tear down a house into the tiniest pieces so that no one would ever know that those pieces once made a house. But each piece, even one as small as an atom, would have a place. God would be the Place that contained all of the tiny bits, just as God was their Place when they were combined into a house. And that is why, in a particularly lovely way, Yona can know that when she and her mother go their separate ways each morning, God is with them both.

God and Mystery

3

The term "mystery," which had been used to describe some pagan religions of the rabbinic period and which became highly significant in Christian theology, never really had a major place in discussions of Jewish belief. That is, I think, because biblical Judaism, and therefore the rest of our religious tradition, is centrally built on revelation—God's talking to people about what God has done, will do, or wants Jews to do.

Nonetheless, amid all this communication from God to people, there is a sense that there is something about God that is necessarily hidden from us. The Bible refers to this aspect in picturesque terms such as thick darkness or radiant glory: the awesome greatness that makes God close, yet unapproachable. No wonder the prophet Isaiah saw celestial seraphim, angels, cover their faces; the Torah says flatly that people cannot see God's "face" (that is, God's "self") and survive. Jews know enough about God to know that God is utterly beyond us, what theologians term "transcendent." Thus despite all God has told us, there is also much about God we don't and can't know, and it is this sensibility that prompts Jewish thinkers today to talk about the mystery of God.

I'd say that Jews, regardless of their religious underpinnings, think about and discuss God in three different ways. After all, our denominations resulted not from their distinctive views of the nature of God, but from their disagreement about what God requires of us today. As a result, we may find representatives of these three ways of speaking about the Unknowable Known One among the Law bound as well as among those whose view of Torah is strongly evolutionary.

I'll term these divergent perspectives rationalist, mystic, and relational. The rationalist and mystic views each categorically reject the approach of the other but have similarly grand goals concerning how much we need to know about God. They both want to know everything knowable about God, differing only on the extent to which this is possible. The rationalists seek to know all that reason allows a rational person to know about God and, faithful to that goal, spurn every effort to go beyond what the mind can logically validate.

The mystics have a similarly strong view of what we need to know about God but believe that mystic experience can open up God's innermost being to the dedicated adept. Kabbalistic masters are breathtakingly specific about God's quintessential nature. God is the Absolutely Unlimited, *En Sof,* and thus nothing at all may properly be said of God (not even this). But God is simultaneously the ten emanations or *s'firot,* the interrelated nodes of God's power and functioning that may be "understood" via mystical experience and expressed in almost unlimited symbolism. Thus, while rationalists overcome God's mysterious unknowableness by limiting religiosity to what a logical mind can properly know, the mystics teach us how to expand our comprehension so that at our best, we might momentarily become one with God, and in this state live the Divine mystery.

Proponents of the third, relational point of view (where I would locate myself and most Jewish feminist thinkers) believe that rationalists settle for too little of God, while the mystics reach for too much. Each turns to a special way of knowing to unravel the mystery: the one, by modeling itself after the strict proofs of geometry; the other, by seeking ecstasy, the rising up out of oneself. By contrast, everyday experience teaches us how we can live responsibly amid the jumble of the known and unknown. Falling in love—better, staying in love—is the classic case. As deeply as we have come to know our love, we realize that much about the person will remain a mystery to us, hence the famous premarriage jitters. Yet it is to just this person that we now pledge our lives. This odd mix of understanding and not understanding does not change much through the years; if anything, experience only magnifies the mystery of who our partner really is and explains why we continually rededicate ourselves to keeping the mystery of our love alive.

Building a relationship with God is something like that, though it certainly involves much greater not-knowing. We at least can claim to have firm knowledge of another human, since he or she is so like us. God—being One, unique, incomparable—isn't. We know enough about God to know that God has endowed us with sufficient godliness that we can have some feel for Who or What God is, and for what we at our best may become. Perhaps that is why the Torah, as our liturgy reminds us, commands us to love God rather than try to comprehend God logically. Jews who feel this relational way live with a fluctuating mixture of mystery and intimacy with God.

I see no means by which we may resolve this difference of belief. More important, I think Judaism has been right over the years to leave this theological issue and others like it open, thereby allowing Jews of differing sensibilities to find their place in our community. In working out our Covenant with God, our people has on the whole been convinced that we can know a good deal more about what God wants us to do than about Who or What God really is or how God "works" in the universe.

By creating various styles of fulfilling our duties to God by means of the diverse social orders in which we find ourselves, rather than by our theologies, the leaders of Judaism have created a form of spirituality through the centuries to characterize themselves as a people of faith.

But personal tragedy and social outrage have often made this difficult indeed, and recent history has overwhelmed many a devout soul. I will discuss the various Jewish theological responses to the problem of evil elsewhere in this book. Here, let me add only what neighborly concern and pastoral experience regularly teach: When tragedy strikes, it is the demonstrated love of attentive friends and caring community that begins the healing of the wounded heart. A time will come when we are ready to reflect on what it all might mean, and only then will theology be able to bring its comfort.

The Many Meanings of "God Is One"

4

No traditional Jewish statement about God comes closer to the literal truth than the central affirmation of Jewish faith, the Shema: God is One. But like all great symbols, the surface simplicity that so enhances its appeal also conceals layers of meaning, which together turn out to be quite complex. "The Lord is One"—*Adonai echad*—conveys not just one idea about God, but many, all at once. Let us play a semantic game to see how many common English uses of the word "one" can provide insight into the Jewish understanding of God. Here are some examples.

- "As easy as one, two, three." "One" here means the first of a series, the beginning of the whole thing. Furthermore, it is the generator of the rest of the series, since we add "one" to get the next "one"—but the first "one" never loses its identity in getting us to two or three or four. It stays "one."
- "It's the first one." In this usage, "one" points to what is primary in a series or a group. If you lost or took away this "one," the others would collapse—it is that fundamental to the others.
- "And that makes one." We know that something isn't partial or incomplete, merely a fraction of what we are creating or searching for. It is whole, with all the positive qualities that signify not needing or missing anything.

- "All those tendrils come from one vine." Here we can see how things are linked to one another. Instead of being several different things, "they" form a single unit. This "one" integrates the pieces, giving it a singular, specific character, even though we might believe it consists of separate, discrete parts. Here, "one" testifies to what brings the many together to create a whole.

- "No, it's just one ————." Someone may insist that there are all sorts of impurities or contaminants in this object. We reply that it's basically a single piece of chocolate or one multifaceted emerald. The oneness in this case is a matter of quality and purity or, if you wish, simplicity.

- "She's one of the trustees." Now we are specifying membership in a certain group, the oneness that testifies to identity. If someone doesn't have it (whatever "it" is in this situation) or has it mixed up with something else, "one" cannot be included in this group.

- "You're the one." On the other hand, here we are stating that you are unique—literally, "uni," the one—the exclusive item of this kind. This can also be parsed as "alone." In declarations of admiration or love, "one" points to the absence of any second or third of similar status to the "one."

- "In this field you're number one." We have reversed the number series and are counting backward, reaching to a limit with the "one," the highest position or status in this series, after which there is no other (such as a Top Ten list). To be supreme is to be utterly alone, with all the rest inferior to you.

- "Let's get together one day next week." We can also use "one" to be quite indefinite about things. Is uniqueness something that can't be pinned down? We know it is out there, but it has some elusiveness about it, leaving us with enough knowledge to talk about but not enough to specify what "it" is.

- "But one Wednesday each month I preach." The previously open-ended "one" is now a specifying "one," as happens, say, when we shift from "one rabbi" to "one Rabbi Borowitz" and not any other in this group.

• "The rabbis and the laity are one." Here we suddenly shift from mathematical metaphors to a much desired human value, peace. On occasion we have all been in groups where our views set us apart from other positions being voiced; we could describe such discussions as fragmented. What an achievement, then, to turn clashing opinions into genuine agreement, what the psalmist characterized as brothers [people] living together in unity, "*shevet achim gam yachad*" (Psalm 133:1).

A fitting conclusion to this imaginative thinking is a cryptic statement from the Book of Zechariah that finishes the recitation of the Aleinu prayer, which concludes Jewish services with a vision of humankind's full acceptance of God: "On that day *Adonai* will be one and [*Adonai's*] name will be one" (14:9). "On that day" refers to the messianic time when God will bring all humankind to acknowledge and live by *Adonai's* rule. To me, this also points to an unprecedented unity, a time when God's reality and what people say of God will finally be *echad*, identical, a messianic state indeed.

5

Is Our God Experience Authentic?

Directly stated, there is no infallible way to know whether we have had an authentic encounter with God. In other words, when we reflect on our sense that God was present to us, we probably remember feeling a certain confidence, perhaps one accompanied by an aura of well-being—although the tone may also be one of skepticism rather than assurance. If we regularly guard against being taken in by our own emotions or by spurious others, we may come away from any intimations of the holy feeling quite dubious, or even the opposite! With fraudulent gurus abounding and all sorts of spiritual leaders promising to assuage our anxieties, most of us are more gullible than we readily admit. What might have first seemed like religious truth may on second look be something quite different.

It would be nice if Jewish tradition supplied a foolproof way to keep us from error in matters of religious experience; unfortunately, in this case the tradition can take us only so far. For example, there have been two major schismatic groups that perverted Jewish belief: the ninth-century Karaites and their successors, who rejected rabbinic teaching; and the followers of Shabbatai Zvi, whom many Jews considered the Messiah even after he converted to Islam, in the seventeenth century.

The Torah's words about distinguishing between true and false prophets are of limited help. They advise us that if what was predicted comes true, we were indeed dealing with a true prophet. We can't do much with such after-the-fact confirmation these days, since prophecy has long since ceased among us.

Far more useful is the test applied by the Rabbis to those they suspected of being the Jewish equivalent of heretics. The most famous case is their early second-century archvillain, Elisha ben Abuyah. Once a noted rabbi and the cherished teacher of the famous Rabbi Meir, ben Abuyah was excommunicated, put in *herem*, by his rabbinic colleagues after he espoused a type of paganism. When his beliefs led him to stop observing Jewish law, the Rabbis knew he had left their covenanted community and gone to an "evil" way of life. While liberal Judaism today is not as law bound as were the Rabbis, most Jews would agree that the best evidences of an authentic encounter with God are the actions that such an encounter prompts.

A second, subtle indicator of an authentic meeting between a Jewish person and God is that it changes our relationship with the Jewish religious community. Of course, having a sense that one has been close to God, even momentarily, changes us personally. But for all that God is involved with us individually, our God has been concerned with the Jewish people for millennia. As valuable as you and I are as individuals, God didn't give the Torah to us merely as a self-help manual. A genuine encounter with God should deepen our participation in communal Jewish religious life as well as its ethical outreach. For some people, that may mean adopting more traditional practices; but it may well encourage others to seek newer ways of piety. If it was truly God we connected with, we will want to build on and enhance that experience.

Something similar can be said of a third indicator, that we will want to know more of what the Jewish tradition has taught about what defines a worthy relationship with God. One important feature is to be open to what contemporary Jewish religious teachers are saying. God being so great, there is considerable variety in not only the views of the teachers but also in their ways of expressing their personal meetings with the Sacred. Music and poetry, new rituals and reinterpreted old ones, may deepen their and our own realizations of the Presence.

In such matters, it is good to have a learned Jew as your guide. In most cases, this will be a trusted rabbi; however, it could be any Jew whose character, actions, and knowledge of Judaism significantly exceeds your own. If you don't have such a spiritual companion, let me urge you to begin the process of finding one.

All this will, I hope, help you find your Jewish religious way, yet there are no fail-safe guarantees whenever the heart or the soul is involved. Though you may bring high emotion and deep searching to your critical decisions about love, marriage, divorce, or other life-shaping matters, you can never be sure you have not gone wrong.

A religious ceremony performed during the Jewish Day of Atonement, Yom Kippur, may bring comfort to our disturbing inability to find complete certainty. Rabbinic traditions recount what the high priest had to do in the Temple each Yom Kippur before he acknowledged to God the transgressions of the people. At this climactic religious moment, in front of everyone, the high priest had to first confess his and his family's "sins, iniquities, and transgressions." Similarly, today at the beginning of the Yom Kippur evening service, the clergy come before the open ark and first plead for forgiveness of their sins before leading the congregation in our own confessions.

Of course it would be nice to live a risk-free life, but Judaism teaches that no one, not Moses, not the high priest, ever lived flawlessly. No one can guarantee that what we have experienced with God is with the One God of the universe. But situating ourselves within the Jewish people's vast experience with God should provide the best available direction.

The Jewish Idea(s) of God

6

Now it seems clear that Judaism requires a belief in God—but why do the intellectual streams of twenty-first-century Judaism travel in such wide and diverse paths just to say what that idea should be? To help answer that question, or perhaps rethink it, the classic Jewish response to such issues needs to be understood. That understanding begins by asking some tough questions. How will we recognize a reasonably authentic Jewish idea of the Eternal One when we find it? What criteria should we employ to determine whether one theory or another will best assist us in reaching a correct answer? And what gives me the right to tell other Jews how to deal with this crucial matter?

The last question is the easiest one to answer. No, I don't have any special Jewish authority on this issue. I do bring my long years of study and thinking about these subjects to what I say. Nonetheless, as the answer to the first question will make plain, if what I present doesn't make good sense, there is certainly no Jewish obligation to believe it.

It will help us understand the particularly Jewish way of thinking about God if we begin our analysis with a brief look at how other religions have dealt with this question. In Christianity, not just a general belief in God but one's specific idea of God is crucial. The apostle Paul made faith in the crucified and risen Jesus central. By professing faith in Jesus as Christ, or savior, a person becomes and lives as a Christian and achieves salvation. Other religions subscribe to far different beliefs. For Theravadin Buddhism, which claims to be the oldest Buddhist tradition, any idea of God is irrelevant. Its chief concern is the universal suffering of humanity; its goal, to overcome that suffering. So this type of Buddhism has no idea of God because it has no place for God in its faith agenda.

If Christianity focuses upon redemption from sin and Buddhism is devoted to release from suffering, what is Judaism centered upon? What is the axis, the pivot of the Jewish religion? For me, the root religious experience of Judaism is not the negative escape from sin or suffering. It is the positive hearing of *Adonai*'s commands to serve as a people and as individuals devoted to creating a world reflecting God's holiness. It is the sense that God wants humankind to act in God-like ways. It is the feeling for mitzvah (commandment, or good deed). It is Torah.

Theoretically, one might say that Torah is pure form, the continuous commitment to mitzvah that the people of Israel, in response to God, learn and seek to live by. It is to this, to the never-ending effort to make more precise how God would have us spend our days, that the Jewish mind has dedicated itself. Thus we should not be surprised that it was in this area of Torah that Judaism chose to make exacting decisions and to exercise religious discipline—what our tradition calls halachah (law). The rigor of halachah is the closest that Judaism comes to the authority of Christian dogma. Our halachic codes of law are Judaism's closest compilations to Christian creed.

But halachah is clearly limited to questions of action; halachah does not embrace the field of thought. Ideas of God are located in another sphere of discourse, the sphere of Torah the Rabbis called the aggadah, all rabbinic teaching that is not legal. Halachah strives for completeness and precision; aggadah surrenders these and strives instead for partial illumination and brief insight into the whole. Halachah seeks to resolve opposing views; aggadah is quite tolerant of apparent contradictions. In aggadah, Jews search for ever more adequate expressions of the meaning of *Adonai*. Jews may spend their whole lives in this quest. Judaism has given to aggadah, its world of ideas, extraordinary freedom.

For example, according to halachah, the legal time limit for flour and water to be transformed into kosher matzah for Passover is eighteen minutes. Any longer and the matzah is *t'reif*, or not kosher. In contrast, the aggadist Rabbi Levi, basing himself on 1 Kings 21:25, spent six months preaching about King Ahab's sinfulness: "Indeed, there never was anyone like Ahab, who committed himself to doing what was displeasing to the Lord" (1 Kings 21:25a). But Ahab visited Rabbi Levi in a dream, reminding him that, according to the last half of the biblical verse, Ahab's sinning was "at the instigation of his wife Jezebel" (1 Kings 21:25b). Taking advantage of the freedom of the *aggadah*, Rabbi Levi then spent six months expounding Ahab's virtues—aggadic freedom indeed!

Placing the idea of God in the realm of halachah would have meant that Judaism believed the human mind capable of reaching as authoritative decisions about God as about mitzvah. The Torah says of the commandment that it is neither too hard for us nor too far for us (Deuteronomy 30:11). Judaism maintains that halachah is clearly within our power to understand and determine. Yet the Torah does not speak this way of *Adonai*. Indeed, the Torah emphasizes the opposite, that though we may know the will of *Adonai*, we "may not see God's face and live" (Exodus 33:20).

Judaism purposely confines the idea of God to the realm of aggadah because it knows the limits of human reason. For in Judaism, we conclude, all efforts to speak of God, all of Jewish theology, must be conducted in freedom. Thus it is a contradiction of our tradition to speak of "the" Jewish idea of God. Judaism has but one God, but not one idea of *Adonai*.

For Judaism, God's holiness is revealed most clearly in sacred living and in the open pursuit of ever less inadequate terms, enabling us to draw ever closer to the One we know well enough to know is ever beyond full knowing.

———————————————

7

Relating to God: Substance or Style?

I don't blame people for being confused by the contrary ways that those in a given Jewish group—in my case, Reform Judaism— claim to earnestly respond to God. I believe I can rather quickly clear up one of the common difficulties about that, but another is too complex for a simple answer, though I'll do my best with it.

Some people were troubled initially by the contrast between the Reform rabbis' 1999 statement about their movement's basic beliefs about God and most actual Reform worship these days. They found the Pittsburgh Principles, as the document is generally called, abstract and somewhat "cool" about God, while the liturgical style in most temples is rich with emotion and body language, more an exercise in feeling than in intellect. If that isn't an outright contra- diction, it certainly seems to be a disturbing move from beliefs to consequences.

However, the alleged clash between the statement and our actual practice is in fact due to the different religious tasks each is seeking to achieve. The first—the statement of faith—seeks to explain and speaks mainly to the mind; the second—the prayer service—seeks to express mainly what we feel in God's presence. I suppose we could try to accomplish our pronouncement by creating an exqui- site poem that made plain what we ultimately care about, and the greatest psalms do something like that. But if a religious document seeks to make belief reasonably clear, it will stick to prose and hope that, on occasion, it may soar.

Liturgy doesn't aim to obscure, only to recognize that much of what we "know" or "feel" transcends words. It therefore specializes in activities beyond talk—in sacred space (the difference in a synagogue between the foyer and the sanctuary, or between the closed and the open Ark), musical instruments, song, chant, *niggun* (wordless singing), and, best of all, many think, in silence. The Bible also mentions clapping, shouting, arm waving, and even fully prostrating oneself before *Adonai*. The same One God may properly be addressed using either prose or poetry. Surely Judaism ought to have a place for simple, clear exposition of what we believe, as well as for our ongoing efforts to stay in touch with God and to celebrate our continued relationship.

What is not as easy to explain is the radical shift in tone and style of Reform and other Jewish worship in recent times. We may, with more imagination than data, characterize it this way: Years back, we came to the synagogue expecting an impressive service that, at its formal best, radiated a sense of awe in the presence of God. While I am not suggesting this has completely disappeared, our prayers these days are largely exercises in congregational self-expression. There is a lot of congregational singing, often to new compositions that are richly rhythmic and melodic, and many fewer moments when the rabbi or the cantor is the center of the service. Except for the High Holy Days and other special occasions, people may dress quite casually. With emphasis on prayers for the sick and similar participation, there is often a palpable sense of the sacred. How much of this mood arises from a sense of Jewish togetherness or from a parallel sense of the people's Covenant with God cannot easily be determined.

What makes this difference so difficult to discuss with partisans of either style—groups generally separated by a considerable age gap—is the mix of personal taste and relationship to God that lies at its heart. Let me illustrate with an example that may say more about my age than about my good judgment. It has to do with how we dress when we come to synagogue. During my youth, when my family went to services, we did so with an air of respect for our temple and, less consciously but truly, with a certain reverence for God. Our clothes and deportment reflected that we were going to an important meeting. I may have been uncomfortable in my dress shoes and clothes, and I certainly disliked wearing a tie that threatened strangulation, but that was beside the point: Going to synagogue was an important event, and God had to be treated with proper respect. A generation earlier, though males sat with uncovered heads, females wouldn't dream of going to temple without wearing hats and gloves—and children's shoes, not sneakers or flipflops, were polished. The formality of this older style has now largely been replaced by greater congregational casualness, but with increased congregational involvement.

I think the more formal religious style had more to do with postimmigrant adaptation to America than it did with theology. We got a measure of quiet self-satisfaction from the sense that our Christian neighbors approved of the etiquette of our modernized Judaism. The godliness that sometimes more, sometimes less, accompanied this liturgical practice was also more evident then. That generation's favorite biblical verse, the one everybody knew and considered almost a second Shema, was, "It hath been told thee, oh man, what is good and what the Lord doth require of thee: only to do justly, to love mercy and to walk humbly with thy God" (Micah 6:8). Our piety in those days came out most clearly in the ethical living, social concern, and humane idealism people were expected to manifest, and it was reinforced by our strong condemnation of Jews who deviated from that creed.

I am saying that though the more outward-extending, formally religious style of yesteryear was quite different from today's more inward-extending, informal piety, many Jews then took their religion just as seriously. And how peoples' lives were affected, not one manner of religiosity or another, certainly seems to be the point. We need to care less about religious style and more about just how significant God is in our lives.

If God is indeed the One, Ultimate source of goodness and value in the universe, we personally and our community as a whole ought to stay in touch with God continually. As one Talmudic Rabbi distilled it, a caring Jew should say a hundred blessings each day, not just those of the daily services but all those acknowledgments—for bread, for something new, for being able to go to the toilet—that recognize God's ongoing goodness to us (Menachot 43b). And even those of us who only have a passing sense that God is near ought to find a way, in whatever style, of cultivating a serious, personal relationship by regularly acknowledging the Presence. As the psalmist put it, "I set *Adonai* before me continually. With God at my right hand, I shall not be shaken" (Psalm 16:8).

8

Accepting the World God Willed

The self looms so large in today's American psyche that religious life must largely devote itself to explaining and exemplifying how observance enables us to attain our personal goals. One might well fantasize the task of the Jewish clergy as continually seeking new ways to satisfy a community that prays with its spiritual remote control ever at the ready. Even employing this strategy in small, responsible doses will not help much when it comes to explaining what saying Kaddish Yatom, the mourner's version of the Jewish prayer elaborately praising God, might mean to us.

Just a few generations back, things were different. Most people believed that saying the prayer eased the fate of their loved ones in the Jewish version of purgatory. Those who doubted the prayer's power to relieve had another motive for saying it—they did not want others in their small communities to consider them neglectful of their proper duties to the dead.

Today those motives for saying Kaddish have been pretty well lost. Even reducing the acceptable standard for mourners from daily recitation to doing so at the weekly Shabbat service has not resuscitated the old pattern. Families often limit themselves to the Shabbat service after the funeral.

That being the case, I do not propose now to remedy this lapse in our mourning rites by offering a creative rationale for why saying Kaddish is good for the mourner. Rather, as I learned myself during my mourning year for my wife, if we can move beyond self-concern and attend to what the Kaddish prayer is saying to God and to us, we can discover what Jewish tradition wisely teaches us about reshaping our goals after our loss.

The basic Kaddish text, the so-called half Kaddish or Hatzi Kaddish, consists of only three sentences plus another said by the congregation. In the mourner's version, the Kaddish Yatom, two sentences are added that look forward to the establishment on earth of God's all-embracing peace.

One can easily be confused about the ending of the first sentence, because when the worshippers hear the words *Sh'mei Rabbah,* "the Great Name," a euphemism for the Tetragrammaton (the four-letter name, YHVH, that by long custom is never to be pronounced), they interrupt the sentence with a rousing "amen." The thought, however, continues for three critical, additional words. Translating the Kaddish into English is frustrating, since most of its Aramaic has no good English equivalent. If some fractured English is allowed, I can convey its meaning in this way: "May the Great Name—[God's]—be 'greater-ed' and 'holy-ed'—[magnified and sanctified]—in the world which 'He'—[God]—created according to 'His'—[God's]—will." The prayer's unambiguous, repetitive theme is God's transcendence.

There is a telling ambiguity in the way the prayer's many verbs, here and particularly in its paragraph-length third sentence, resonantly convey this. They are in what is known as the *hitpael* form, which translates as either the reflexive or passive voice, with the latter the one adopted by almost all translations. But the reflexive possibility suggests that for all our mortal efforts to ascribe appropriate greatness and sanctity to God, it is *Adonai* alone who might adequately do so. God's nearness inevitably reveals God's "far-ness" from us, which makes it breathtaking that the Beyond-Us-One elects to covenant with humankind.

What deeply jolted me during my many recitations of the prayer was the first sentence's concluding phrase. Standing there dutifully, often barely containing my resentment that death, God's creation, had taken Estelle from me, I found myself required to praise God *b'olmah divra chirutei*, "in the world that God created according to God's will."

Those words hit me hard. Typical American that I am, I want the world to have been created for my sake, or at least for the fulfillment of my worthy purposes. I certainly didn't want it to inevitably and irrevocably snatch away the one I loved. But the rabbinic authors of the text, so often my teachers, insisted that the world was created as an effect of God's *r'utei*, the Aramaic of the more familiar Hebrew *r'tzono*, "His [God's] will"—a world not created as I might have wanted it but according to God's *ratzon*, God's will. Like honor (*kavod*) and blessed (*baruch*) and other such God-terms, *ratzon* strains to describe an aspect of God that both is familiar and yet soars beyond us.

An analogy may make this less murky. When we speak of God's will, we seek to describe something beyond our understanding, yet apparently true to God's nature or activity. Like other theological terms, the notion of God's will is borrowed from our experience in human relationships. We all have had a boss or friend whom we thought we understood well, yet who one day did something quite unexpected. If it is far out of the other's character as we knew it, we may say the action was willful, that is, proceeding not from the orderly, comprehensible part of the person, but from a personal depth that is true to their nature, yet totally beyond our ken.

Those whose relationship with God is as robust as their concern for self may find this teaching highly significant. I did. It reminded me to stop expecting the world to be designed for my satisfaction and to stop being resentful when it turned out not to be. And it spurred me to be grateful for God's gifts of breath and taste and excretion and thought and energy and a hundred other things for which Jews daily say blessings.

Surely one of the greatest blessings is that human beings were created to have a unique intimacy with God and cooperate with God's purposes, turning this nearness into a sacred act. Saying Kaddish meaningfully instructs us to let God be God. Saying Kaddish brings on the slow healing of God's covenanting nearness.

II
Doing Holy Deeds

9

Being Close to God

A few weeks after the High Holy Days, my eldest daughter, Lisa, serving as president of Congregation Kol Ami in White Plains, New York, described a deeply touching ritual that for the first time at her synagogue had been added to N'ilah, the Yom Kippur concluding service. A Kol Ami congregant had seen a story in *Reform Judaism* magazine about a very different High Holy Days experience. At the beginning of N'ilah, the rabbi announced that the ark would remain open for the entire service. While the rest of the congregation continued to pray, anyone who wished could come up to the ark for some private time with God. Not knowing what to expect from such a radical ritual departure, the rabbi was pleasantly surprised by the steady stream of congregants who participated.

The clergy of Lisa's congregation decided to try the same practice, and though she was ready to help break the ice, her efforts were not needed. It did not take long before a respectable number of people had lined up to have a few private moments before the open ark. Lisa said that afterward, the whole congregation seemed particularly moved by this addition to the service.

I was surprised and thrilled that something that depended on individual religious spontaneity could take place in even two Reform congregations. The old, established custom brought individuals to the ark only when ceremoniously called to perform a ritual. In this case, only a general invitation had been issued, and the response came from personal initiative, for a personal purpose. I was deeply moved to hear of the participants' evident religiosity. So in due course I suggested to the ritual committee chair and to the rabbi of my synagogue, Temple Sinai in Stamford, Connecticut, that we might want to try something similar during our own Yom Kippur services. They were agreeable but felt it would be most meaningful if it were done as a transition to our afternoon service. So, prompted only by an announcement during morning worship, we allowed about fifteen minutes for our ark to remain open for personal prayer, while music played to encourage the rest of the congregation to meditate from their seats. I was astounded when, just as had happened at Lisa's temple, we had quite a number of folks forming a respectful queue to experience their few moments before the open ark.

I share this because what happened has completely contradicted my previous experiences and consequent expectations. For most of the six-plus decades during which I have either led or attended High Holy Day services, the worship has been profoundly formal. People may have relaxed a little in recent years; however, once the service began, the mood was clearly decorous. What's more, many of the people I've met in the community have assured me that they were "not very religious" at all. At best, most of them, if pressed, would say that they would be willing to believe in God if someone could give them a good reason to believe. So far, no one has. Through my long rabbinic life I have taken for granted that most American Jews (and not a few of their rabbis) were fervently agnostic.

Yes, there has been considerable change in the Reform community in recent years—more Hebrew, expanded musical participation at services, and the emergence of caring, believing worshippers. But I never imagined that I would see so many congregants who were serious enough about talking to God to leave the anonymous safety of their pews to stand before the open ark. It blew me away then and still does whenever I think about it.

I believe that this phenomenon deals with what students of ritual call "sacred space." On one level, it's quite peculiar to think that God somehow exists more in one spot in the sanctuary than in another. Isn't God everywhere, particularly, as an early nineteenth century Polish Hasidic master, the Kotzker rebbe taught, wherever we let God in? Isn't that the reason why no one thinks that praying in the front pews is more effective than praying in the back of the sanctuary? Then why would people be moved to leave their seats and go up to the open ark to pray?

For me, the answer hinges on a universal experience—sanctity has a logic all its own. We get a brief idea of this when the Torah scroll is carried through the congregation. We touch the Torah mantle with our prayer book or tallit or fingers and then kiss them, thus indirectly kissing the Torah. Our action says we love the Torah, its holiness, its Godliness. Going up to the ark—not at all a common occurrence—intensifies that experience. Common logic aside, we are closer to God there.

Many seem to ignore the fact that the people filling the sanctuary witness their sacred encounter. Is it because they are so full of gratitude for something wonderful that has happened in the past year or will soon take place? More likely, I would guess, they are so deeply troubled that they are willing to expose their feelings to everyone in the synagogue to commune more intimately with God for a few moments. Whatever the motivation, it is most daring to exhibit our soul's yearnings before others.

Temple Sinai in Stamford has a center aisle, which means that people who come down from the ark have to pass the potential scrutiny of any curious onlooker. I admired those who did this and was awed at the most religiosity I had ever seen in a Reform congregation. I couldn't keep from taking an occasional peek at the returnees. Mostly they walked with bowed heads, refusing to make eye contact and break their mood. I loved them all for their courage and devotion.

It is clear that there is a significant minority of believers in the Jewish community. It is time to start paying more attention to them. I do not know whether the people who wanted to get closer to God this past Yom Kippur will again want their few moments before the open ark. Many may feel that what they want to say to God can be as easily said from their seats in the congregation. Yet some of these people have signaled their connection to God, which is strong enough that occasionally they do not mind if other people know their real piety. They and all the other believing Jews in our community deserve our consideration and our respect. Their faith-fulness keeps us true to the Covenant that our forebears made with God at Mt. Sinai and that all later generations of Jews have sought to exemplify. Whether one day you will want to walk up to the ark as part of the holiest observance of the Jewish year, or whether in solitude or in community, whether apparent or unseen, you seek to live up to the glimpses of God that have come your way, you too will be continuing the ancient Sinaitic promise.

10

The Act and Art
of Praying

Prayer can be a problem because it asks us to do two things that diverge. It's like trying to take the advice someone gives us when we are worried about how to behave at an important gathering: "Just be yourself." If we are working hard to "throw ourselves into things," how can we then simply "be ourselves"? Most of us manage to forget ourselves and succeed at some initially frightening task, like giving a talk or playing in an important tournament. That is, we've learned not to take the advice literally, and we've learned the trick of subordinating the self to the task.

In prayer, this means focusing on God, which isn't always easy but can be as simple as saying the old Jewish prayer word for "Hello, God," which is *Baruch,* the first word of all Hebrew blessings—a word so filled with meaning that we translate it as both "praised be" and "blessed be." When overwhelmed by events, even people who normally view faith as only for the weak-minded have been known to say some words of prayer. Less dramatically, if we really want to get to know someone, we must get beyond our usual guardedness and stop worrying about what we look like or how we're doing. Prayer involves just such a change—from the "think-full" to the "thank-full"—moving us forward to the Source of all that is.

In a time less concerned with the self than ours, Jewish teachers devised a means of pointing us to prayer's special provision. For centuries, when someone entered a synagogue, he or she would find above the ark an inscription admonishing: *Da lifne Mi atah omed,* "Know before Whom you stand." It is adapted from the Talmudic master Rabbi Eliezer ben Hyrcanos' instruction to his disciples about praying: "Be solicitous of the honor of your colleagues; keep your children from mental speculation but let them cuddle close to Talmudic scholars; and when you pray, know before Whom you stand. Doing this will win you a share in the world to come" (Babylonian Talmud, B'rachot 28b). Eliezer, of course, said it in the plural, but its anonymous change to the singular teaches Jews an important lesson about praying.

Although Jewish law calls us to pray as members of God's Covenant people, symbolized by the minyan, the prayer quorum of ten, all congregational prayer fundamentally is composed of single individuals joining one to another. The Talmudic motto commandingly bids us to remember that prayer is talking to *Adonai,* the Ultimate One of the universe. And that sense of prayer holds true today no matter whether you think of God as concept, "person," Nature, Transcending Unity, limited or unlimited Power, the most intimate Parent, the feminist Bearer-Nurturer, the Great Whatever, the utterly Unspeechifiable, or some mix of these. No wonder the traditional prayer book (*siddur*) and modern prayer books use so many different euphemisms for "God"!

It helps to contrast prayer-talk with therapy-talk. Both involve the self most intimately, but where therapy focuses on the individual and our relationships, prayer centers on our relationship with The Other, The Ground And Guide Of All Reality. When we act on Rabbi Eliezer's teaching and turn our consciousness to the Exceptional One, we often discover that what we thought "needed to be said" is transformed into "ought to be said" or simply silently understood. When the Rabbis urged us to pray with appropriate direction, *kavanah*, they were pointing us to the place where interplay with our Prayer Partner can occur. I hear this message in the cryptic Hasidic teaching, "I pray that I might be able to pray."

The prayer ideal has its own peculiar dynamic: now richly achieved but mostly only a hint of the holy; now leaving a blessed afterglow but mostly only glimpsing righteous actions; now a blessed confirmation of our lives but mostly only an intimation of the holy. Why can it not be more reliable, or even like those times when something—a congregation's full-throated response, a sublime musical phrase, a sense of the touch from Beyond—overcomes our emptiness? Why cannot the spare resonance of the ordinary—another morning's wake-up thanks, another blessing for a meal—become the sure embrace of the Presence?

While many congregations adorned their sanctuaries with Rabbi Eliezer's words, the home version of the Talmudic dictum is: "I always set *Adonai* before me" (*Shiviti Adonai lenegdi tamid*) (Psalm 16:8). The psalmist called us to do our part to let the prayer meeting take place. The psalmist's counsel to "set *Adonai* before" us is not meant spatially, as if we need to make a niche or altar in order to pray. Rather, it is about our consciousness. Our minds are normally so packed with things we need or want to do that if we don't push those things aside and concentrate on Who we are talking to, we'll soon be saying pious words but thinking about our schedule. That's not proper prayer in any religion. To follow the psalmist's guidance, we must first relegate all the non-gods of daily life to the back of our consciousness. Then we can "set God before us," attend to God's presence and availability. In that mode, with words or without words, real prayer occurs—the worthy goal of all believers.

The mainstream branches of Judaism, however, have seen in their individuality a loving touch of God's oneness. Rather than turn the self to holy-nothingness, they have followed the psalmists' open approach: Do you wish to come into The Presence? No need for priest or place to stand in your way.

Prayer in Judaism is both the easiest of pieties—like thanking God for bread—and the one whose full achievement seems to forever elude us—for our mind often wanders from the service. No wonder the classic Hebrew term for prayer is *avodah*, labor. It is our life's work, the "labor" that gives our life its inestimable worth.

11

Moses' Prayer for Healing–and Ours

Sometimes in the morning when I am saying the Amidah prayer, the central block of petitions of the Jewish daily services, and I mention the names of ill dear ones in the R'faeinu, the blessing for God's healing of the sick, I can't go on. Perhaps someone on my list has taken a turn for the worse, or my years of praying for an afflicted friend have been to no avail, or I suddenly think about someone I no longer mention because of death. A spasm of futility shakes me; only when faith reclaims me am I able to continue.

Thinking about this, I often find myself back at a 1963 meeting of the Central Conference of American Rabbis, the organization for Reform rabbis in the United States. I am trying to persuade my colleagues to replace their increasingly ineffective rationalism with the recognition of the central place of faith in our Judaism. My listeners mostly respond with a mixture of incredulity and disdain—but not a somewhat older colleague. I clearly remember his words. With a barely restrained sarcasm, he says that he doubts I am now ready to recite the R'faeinu prayer rather than relying on medical science. He was, of course, skewering me for daring to breach the sturdy firewall that then separated the medical clinic and the synagogue.

I never had the opportunity—or was it the nerve?—to ask him some decades later how he viewed what has now become a common worship ritual. Today we offer prayers for healing in virtually all liberal congregations. Today our congregations are filled with voices petitioning God for *r'fuah sh'leimah*, a complete restoration of health.

What brought about this radical change? Of course it isn't that we believe a few heartfelt words will result in a miracle of biblical proportions, as happened to the prophetess Miriam after her brother Moses prayed for her cure. This effective supplication, the most famous one in the Bible, was a mere five-word, six-syllable plea that his sister be cured of leprosy: "Please, God, please heal her" (*El na refa na lah*) (Numbers 12:13).

No, the interruptions in my morning prayer have nothing to do with my inability to bring about a miracle. Something else is involved. I think I can best explain it by relating how our religiosity has evolved in the years since my rabbinic colleague smugly claimed that modernity had subordinated religion in its certainties.

Half a century ago, every college-trained mind knew that God could not act in nature. God might still be invoked to explain our universe's origin, order, and values but not as actually *doing* anything. So it made no sense to ask God to heal. Yet today such certainty seems naive. The old air of omniscience that had permeated the scientific disciplines, including medicine, has largely disappeared. Physicians rarely affect the aura of gods; in fact, many now admit to the usefulness of what once were labeled "alternative forms of treatment."

Although the child in me still wants my doctor to tell me exactly what ailment I have, what will cure it, and how long until the cure kicks in, the adult in me responds best to a caring discussion of my prognosis. I hasten to add that I am not discrediting medical science—I am far too grateful for the eleven pills a day that are keeping me reasonably healthy. I am only pointing to the current prevalence today of accepting a cure that may lack scientifically proven authority. And that brings me back to what lies behind our prayers for healing.

Our shift in recent decades is largely founded on a new humility about what we can really know. One effect has been a new openness to the possibility of God's active role in healing. Judaism these days involves a significant dose of spirituality, a personal quest leading to experiencing the presence of God. This requires neither pooh-poohing science nor kowtowing to it. Hesitantly we shed our old sense of certainty and quietly seek meaning even in our doubting. As new insights guide us, we turn to God as we search for what *Adonai* might independently do. More often than we would ever have imagined, we find that God heals in ways we must call God's own.

As far back as the Bible, we read that one of God's roles is to serve as the Ultimate Therapist: "I, *Adonai*, am your healer" (Exodus 15:26). Biblical faith lived side by side with a devotion to doctors and doctoring. Later, in the Talmud, the Rabbis ruled that physicians are commanded to do their best to heal. Many a Talmudic Rabbi was also a powerful healer. Even today, traditional Jewish law requires the clergy to consult with medical experts when addressing a bioethical question.

In short, the traditional Jewish theology of medicine is dialectical. That is, there are two effective yet seemingly opposing energy sources in the universe: God and people. God, being God, may act independently. People, having only a derivative status, may not. At our best, we act with God; however, the way human and divine energies intertwine is beyond our understanding. It is this all-too-human failure to "know," to comprehend fully how this system works, that occasionally draws me up short as I say prayers for the ill. I'd really like to know exactly how the Divine-human interaction operates. More truthfully, I'd like to know why I don't get the response I want when I have prayed for it so fervently.

I suppose I could end my momentary distress by acknowledging that God, like everything else, has limits. But that makes too much of me and too little of God. Or, like the Jewish mystics and those of many other religions who believe that there only is God, recognize that everything else is illusion. I could then end the problem by learning how to overcome my imagined identity and merge with the One and Only Reality, God. But as I read the Jewish tradition and my self, such a solution makes so much of God that it makes too little of me. So I live with the God whose greatness I sense in all the little healings of each day and therefore trust, even when God does not do all I have asked for.

12

How Shall We Comfort the Mourner?

After my wife, Estelle, died, I received several hundred condolence cards and letters, most of them handwritten. Having myself often sat, ready to set down a few words of comfort but unable to find something that would freshly speak to what the bereaved was going through, I thought I appreciated how little any of us can say in such missives. Still, I was not prepared for the consolation that these messages brought me. So many people, some well remembered, others requiring a real memory search, and still others unknown to me—friends of my children? professional colleagues of my wife's? people I had once taught or otherwise been in touch with?—reached across my new sense of void and sought to bring me back into life.

I will always remain grateful to them. In one sense that is because, early on, I intuited that one way I needed to mourn was to sit hour after hour at my desk and respond, however briefly, to each one in as personal a way as I could. That meant not letting myself merely transcribe the same few ritual phrases, but struggling again and again to find some words faithful to what I was feeling as I wrote. I sometimes failed to live up to this impractical ideal, but mostly I came close enough to bring myself a measure of peace.

With all of that, two things about this process came to trouble me, the one trivial, the other sufficiently disturbing. The slight one was occasioned by the few messages that came by e-mail. Try as I did to think of them as this generation's way of speedily staying in touch, I found it difficult to avoid their impersonality, even when I knew the sender reasonably well. And I never felt comfortable either responding in kind, as I did with some, or responding by hand, as I did with others.

The more disquieting one simply forced itself upon me. Reading and responding to the scores of messages from my colleagues in the clergy, I was shocked that they were overwhelmingly secular. They wrote about my wife living on in memory, or the immortal power of love, or the lasting effect of her good deeds, or the tribute I would render her by turning back to life.

While I do believe in all these commonplaces of American condolence, now, face-to-face with her death, what I needed was at least a touch of the sacred. Many Jews pride themselves on being more spiritually alive today, but when it came to consoling me about my wife's death, most said nothing about God. Only a few felt comfortable in speaking to me of God's healing presence, or of what faith in God means in the face of death, or, harder still, what it might mean to affirm God's sovereignty when understanding fails us.

Please do not misunderstand me. I was not looking for a theological essay. A felt sentence, a suggestive phrase or two, anything that pointed me to the Divine Otherness would have fulfilled the promise of my years of Jewish practice, of the services, study, and ritual that have long filled my life with meaning. I could not reconcile the lack of references to God with the constant news that ours is a time of increased spirituality, when people seek to open themselves to God's presence in the everyday and the ordinary.

Why, then, did so many clergy revert to the human aspects of death and mourning instead of pointing even hesitantly to the God who might be close by, if only we could summon the courage to reach for God's "hand"?

Reticence is not misplaced when it comes to comforting the mourner. Too much talk can easily become oppressive. A flood of words, however well intentioned, can appear blasphemous, as even talk of a "good death" flies in the face of our good God Whom we daily praise for giving us life. And when we, the living, are stricken with a bruising, crushing death, the wisdom of Jewish tradition that counsels us to refrain from speaking until first spoken to by the mourner is clearly comprehensible.

Nonetheless, mourners need some "rod and staff" to comfort them, some word or gesture that the Shepherd indeed is leading them through this dark, dark valley. It would have been a soothing balm to hear the leaders of our liturgy offer even simple prayers like "May God be with you" or "May God's presence enfold you." And I was deeply thankful, therefore, when some such rabbinic spirituality came my way.

13

Traditional Words of Condolence

A good number of colleagues who sent me condolence messages after my wife died closed their messages with the ritual formula: "May God comfort you among all the rest of the mourners of Zion and Jerusalem" (*Hamakom y'nacheim etchem betoch sh'ar aveilei tziyon v'y'rushalayim*). I confess that often the mere sight of these Hebrew words warmed my soul, but I soon became unhappy with the meaning they conveyed.

I decided to do some research to find the origin and likely initial intent of the sentence, and I discovered an impressive book on Jewish consolation practices: Shmuel Glick's *Light and Consolation*. He writes that there is general scholarly agreement that the "mourners of Zion," *aveilei tziyon*, were originally post-Talmudic ascetics dedicated to mourning the destruction of the Temple. When they began this practice is debated, but the surest historical evidence indicates that in the ninth century, Karaites (a break-off Jewish group who rejected rabbinic teachings of the Talmud and lived by biblical teachings only), who came to Jerusalem, created or adopted the name and the ritual. In later centuries the Karaite influence faded, and invoking this formula became a widespread Ashkenazic (relating to Jews of central and eastern European descent) custom.

In recent years, however, taking the statement literally makes little sense. Most modern Jews do not mourn the present physical state of Jerusalem and are unlikely to be bereft at the destruction of the Temple, as the widespread nonobservance of Tisha B'Av (the ninth day of the Hebrew month Av, traditionally a fast day commemorating the destruction of the First and Second Temples and other Jewish calamities) indicates. In the face of this changing belief, the creative power of custom, or *minhag*, has once again made itself felt by understanding the old formula in a new way. The *aveilei tziyon v'y'rushalayim* are now understood to be not a sect but "all Jews who are mourning." Thus the old statement is now taken to mean, "May God console you among all the other Jews who are mourning."

My initial response to this refurbishing was somewhat positive. Mourning is substantially an act of psychic self-defense, even a certain healthy narcissism, so this formula now reminds us that we are not alone. Other Jews are facing their losses amid a community that has long known how to face death and yet affirm life. But I quickly rejected the value of this transformed meaning. Intolerably, it diminished the particularity of my sorrow by seeking to diffuse it in the sea of all other Jewish deaths, advising me to think of my own great loss as one of the other deaths Jews everywhere were mourning. Loyal Jew that I hope I am, I was saying Kaddish for just this particular woman, Estelle Covel Borowitz, and it was precisely the end of my wife's individuality, of her incomparable singularity, that had brought me to be standing there. That being so, it was only in limited ways, as in saying Kaddish at services, that I could tolerate some sense of mourning in general.

Was it some such understanding that prompted a few colleagues to limit their consolatory conclusion to "God will comfort you," *Hamakom y'nacheim etchem*? I found these few words to be a helpful abbreviation of the ritual phrase. It spoke directly of what Jewish religiosity could say to me by speaking of God with a classic term,

"The Place," *HaMakom*, which did not clash with my sensitivity to engendering the Divine. Alas, that very insight quickly pointed me to a new problem: What sense could it make to speak of The Place as a comforter? The very impersonality of this term for God that had made it so attractive now entangled me in the problem of calling on the impersonal One to do the intimately personal act of consoling the mourner.

Should I be so obsessively analytical about ritual? Surely this is not the only case in liturgy where Jews have preferred usage to logical consistency. So, with an occasional wince, I now can live with the abbreviated version of the classic formula. Is that a sufficient consolation, *nechemta*, for all this thinking about what mostly has been simple doing? I do not know, but to paraphrase Rabbi Kahana's notorious declaration, when as a student he hid under his teacher's bed, "It was Torah and I needed to learn it" (Talmud, B'rachot 62a).

14

A New Phase
in Jewish Piety

I want to make the case that much of believing non-Orthodox North American Jewry has moved to a second phase of its piety. The idea that a broad swath of American Jewry is pious will seem quite incongruous to people who still think of Tevya, the famous dairyman-hero from *Fiddler on the Roof,* or a bearded, caftan-clad *yeshiva bocher,* the long, black-coated young male student of an advanced Talmudic academy, as the properly "religious" type. But if piety means taking religion to heart and, in the case of liberal Judaism, trying in our own American way—"Excuse me, Rabbi, but with all due respect, I'd like to make up my own mind about what I'll do"—to live by its teachings, then there have long been significant numbers of pious Jews on this continent.

The first phase of non-Orthodox Jewish piety was accommodationist, finding ways to adjust post-immigrant lives to the openness of a way of life-in-the-making that the still-youthful American democracy was building. So we were dedicated less to ritual than to high human goals of freedom and ethical behavior. With a little stretch, we considered these the critical modern *mitzvot* and a restatement of Judaism's ancient universalism, its teaching about all humankind. We can still find exemplars of this old ethics-first piety in our communities, not the least in complaints about the change in focus and tone (Judaism's embrace of love and joy in its Jewishness) that has come over Jewish life.

Hindsight makes clear the defects of this Americanizing spirituality. If all that really mattered is ethics, why bother about religion? If every thoughtful person has similar goals, why care about being Jewish? And if North American democracy is a sure guide to human flourishing, Zionism (the movement to create a Jewish state, building our lives around its culture) is a diversion, and, in fact, we should substantially reduce distinguishing signs of our Jewishness, such as Hebrew, chanting, and body language.

What primarily doomed that post-ghetto piety was its optimism about humankind. Yes, others had been good enough to give Jews civil rights, but it was then assumed that every educated, cultured person would also be ethical. The twentieth century brutally forced us to confront the human genius for doing evil. Nothing made that clearer than the Holocaust. The "God" we lost in that horror was not *Adonai*—we had long been too agnostic for that belief. The "god" who died for us was the one we had truly believed in—humanity's rationality and ethical competence.

The dizzying passage from the modern to the postmodern turned the old piety upside down. Instead of striving to be simply people who retain some old Jewish roots, most liberal Jews see themselves as Americanized Jews whose old traditions give them a special dedication to human betterment. We notice this in the changed tone of our worship services. Though the patterns vary widely from congregation to congregation, we pray a lot less in English and much more in Hebrew. Our music tends to the participatory—sometimes romantic, sometimes rhythmic. The sermon, once considered the highlight of the service, is now often a relatively brief *d'var Torah*, expounding upon a small portion of the weekly Torah portion, rather than a response to an issue agitating contemporary culture or politics.

We find a similar shift in our theology. Our hard-gained humility about human competence has opened us to spirituality, or, less timidly put, to God. We no longer talk about trying to be hard-headed rationalistic types, but rather easily refer to experience or relationship or even to mysticism. This intellectual change of tone is accompanied by a fresh appreciation of what the classic texts of Judaism can still teach us when read through the lenses of our cultural, sociological, and political emancipation.

Seeing all this, some in the North American Jewish press are apt to state that our liberal community is becoming "more Orthodox." What a senseless charge that is. In most Jewish movements today, women can be ordained rabbis or cantors and come to positions of leadership and influence. Fewer among us deny that the child of a Jewish father, brought up with Jewish study and celebration, is not a legitimate Jew. Our seminaries enroll gay and lesbian students; our synagogues welcome gay and lesbian Jews, and support their civil and Jewish rights to marry.

I should like to see the day when the Jewish press will focus on how much of our North American experimentation has become an accepted part of our community style. Yes, most American Jews have a low number of children, but almost nobody tries to remedy this by telling us it's a mitzvah to procreate. Not many people will listen to such an appeal; instead, people will almost certainly evaluate this and similar proposals in terms of what they personally believe to be their Jewish duty. Ideology may get them to talk about Jewish law, yet when it comes to action they are largely stealth individualists.

Another example of some Jews' failure to acknowledge the positive, modernizing effect of non-Orthodoxy is the trendy Jewish talk about Kabbalah. Its teachers almost never acknowledge that classic kabbalistic books and teachers depict women and feminist qualities as closely associated with human evil. (The exception is the kabbalistic understanding of Shechinah, God's presence, as feminine.) Thankfully the overwhelming majority of Jews today rejects such sexism and won't listen to any teaching that promotes it. So the contemporary proponents of Kabbalah know that they will not win any converts to the old Jewish mysticism unless they radically Americanize it, as they do.

One last example: When nineteenth-century German Jews began to achieve equality with their Christian neighbors, they enthusiastically utilized the vernacular to ensure that modern Jews fully understood Jewish teachings. This practice met fierce opposition from the leading traditionalists of the day, who charged that it would undermine the loyalty of caring Jews. Today a great North American Jewish publisher, whose right-wing Orthodox credentials are impeccable, has been extraordinarily successful precisely because he accompanies his classic Jewish texts with English translations and commentaries. We may be "more Jewish" these days, but we are certainly not turning our backs on what modernization has taught us!

Liberal Judaism's greatest challenge is that in our newfound enthusiasm for our Jewishness, we shall slacken our dedication to mending the world. I am firmly convinced that neither the State of Israel nor the Holocaust nor our focus on our folk particularity, for all their fundamental hold on us, can function as the master narrative of contemporary Jewish existence. Rather I believe that, in an awesome recapitulation of the Exodus, what still most seismically moves us is our emancipation. In becoming equals in the Western world, it was government that was the enabling agent of God's mighty hand and outstretched arm. Therefore when we see governments discriminating against one minority or another, conscience and experience combine to powerfully command us to make government more moral. Any embrace of Jewishness that does not enshrine the recognition that our emancipation radically enlarged our horizon of Jewish religious duty is unworthy of our allegiance. All those pious Jews who know that Torah today demands not only deep Jewish roots but also unending dedication to repairing our shattered world are worthy of God's richest blessing.

15

The Power of Creating
New Religious Customs

Attending a large number of bar and bat mitzvah services in recent years set me to thinking about how non-Orthodox religious sensibility is expressing itself in customs, *minhagim*. While some of these aren't new to American Jews, I was suddenly struck by the number of new synagogue *minhagim* that I don't recall from my early memories of many decades ago.

Two "golden oldies" trace their origin to the largely American creation of the late Friday-evening Shabbat service, itself an accommodation to the realities of the American economic system (just a few generations ago, all Americans had to work long hours, six days a week). The first was the "good-*Shabbos* kiss." Once mixed seating became common in modern synagogues, the end of the service was marked by people saying "good *Shabbos*" to one another, and it soon seemed quite natural to kiss one's spouse. Who knows how many tensions were relaxed by this simple token of affection. In more recent years, it's not only one's own partner on whom one bestows a Shabbat smooch, but many a friend as well. Such community displays of friendliness violate the classic Jewish prohibition against publicly kissing a member of your family and touching someone of the other sex who isn't your spouse. But the Shabbat kiss has by now been long established among non-Orthodox Jews.

A second custom with a vaguely traditional parallel is the after-service *oneg* (meaning "delight," a term used by the prophet Isaiah [58:13] for the Sabbath) *Shabbat*. This, unlike the secular-cultural discussion *oneg* proposed by the early-twentieth-century Hebrew poet Hayim Nachman Bialik, consists of serving coffee and tea plus cakes and cookies to lubricate the schmoozing of worshippers. Of course, the custom may derive from the traditional Kiddush, literally "sanctification." The Kiddush became the name for the cups of wine blessed and drunk by each Jew to sanctify the Sabbath day on its arrival Friday evening and after the Shabbat morning service.

I'm also struck by three other now widely adopted liturgical customs, plus one that has in many places spilled out of the synagogue into life in the larger Jewish community. The first is the widespread custom of offering a prayer in the synagogue for those who are ill, which involves people calling out the names of their stricken friends or loved ones. There is good traditional precedent for this as part of the private prayers associated with the reading of the Torah; however, modernized Jews, in the days when they viewed science as all-knowing, considered such prayers little better than superstition. In recent years, alternative medicine has found a respected place in many a prestigious hospital, so asking God's help for those we love seems only sensible, as attested to by the many names generally volunteered for these prayers. But like the customs mentioned above or noted below, no one quite knows how they got started or how they so quickly established their place in our hearts.

At most of the bar and bat mitzvah services I have been attending, I have been touched by another "modern" custom. Before the Torah is paraded around the sanctuary, the scroll is physically passed down from generation to generation, from the oldest members of the immediate family to one of the parents of the celebrant and then to the child. It seems logical to create an act that makes plain what the morning is all about, namely the passing on of the Jewish tradition to the next generation. The act gives visual testimony not only to the child but also to the family and the congregation assembled with them, emphasizing the meaning behind this celebrative day.

I never can tell what will move me more deeply, either this lovely *minhag* or another that I have encountered now at many bar and bat mitzvah services. In a number of congregations, the child is not only required to manifest considerable ritual literacy, chanting unpunctuated Torah text and making some personal sense of the day's portion, but she or he must have thought of and carried out what is termed a mitzvah project. That involves a creative effort of charity, or *tzedakah*, helping a needy group in the Jewish or general community. I am often overwhelmed by what this child accomplishes to qualify as a maturing Jew. Initiation into our tribe is not only an act of publicly demonstrated bookish Hebraic competence; it also involves an act of caring about and for others. It takes a hard heart to not be in awe of the anonymous Jewish soul who started this practice that many congregations now follow enthusiastically.

A ritual cousin of this practice is the Mitzvah Day program that many congregations and Jewish community centers have made a part of their annual calendar. The sponsoring organization creates a list of helpful acts that people can spend significant time doing that day to further the charitable work of diverse Jewish and non-Jewish groups. The grinch in me grumbles that one should do mitzvot every day of the year, yet I comfort myself with the biblical direction, "So that you may remember and do *all* [my emphasis] My commandments and be holy unto your God" (Deuteronomy 11:13). Or at least try to.

What I find particularly attractive about these customs, these *minhagim*, is that so many Jews have adopted them. The clergy or creative task force can design something they think will be a wonderful addition to the life of their Jewish community, but if people do not embrace it, it joins all those other great activities that haven't survived. But the customs mentioned above seem very much alive. They testify to a quiet but real religious spirit and will stirring in the heart of contemporary American Jewry. As someone who grew up in the days when Jews were mostly concerned with not being "too Jewish," this positive Jewishness moves me greatly.

———————————

16

Fanaticism and Zeal

When people want to attack religion, they inevitably stress how often and how easily "religious fanatics" have incited their followers to do terrible things. The scare words in such charges have been "crusades," "inquisition," and most recently, "jihad." It doesn't seem to make much difference to the accusers that in the last century or so, great human outrages are more likely to have been caused by secular political movements. Those who act with excessive religion, these same indicters state, are particularly culpable for horrible behavior, because they usually claim to be doers of good and proponents of peace. And it is true that, from time to time, persons who claim to be emboldened and empowered by faith will rouse their adherents to inhuman brutality.

Jews, having long suffered from persecution, have a strong survivalist stake in encouraging tolerance and respect from our neighbors. Therefore we often find it difficult to believe that our religion also may incite violence against people who are different from us. However, Jewish tradition provides various grounds for fanaticism. One of the best known is the Torah's account of the zealotry of Pinchas (Numbers 25:6–13). When the Israelites were making their way to the Promised Land, many males allowed themselves to be seduced by local women, not only for sex but also to commit idolatry. One Jew brazenly brought a woman into the holy encampment and took her into his tent. This so incensed the priest Pinchas that he took a spear and skewered the two of them, winning God's special favor for his zealotry.

Two other sources come from the Talmud and later works of Jewish law. One stems from the inexplicable law that Jews may not wear a garment containing both wool and linen. Perhaps because this command is so mysterious, there is a rabbinic dictum that even in the middle of the bustling marketplace, if we see a Jew wearing such a garment, we should summarily rip it off. There is little evidence that this law was ever acted on, although it remains a part of Jewish teaching on appropriate fanaticism. The other rule seems more logical. If one of us sees someone chasing a person in order to commit murder, one may, if necessary to stop the crime, murder the homicidal pursuer. It may be possible to justify such a law as an extension of the practical halachic, or legal, endorsement of self-defense in a period of little community policing. However, this law received a fanatical political reading and became the slayer's justification for assassinating Israeli prime minister Yitzhak Rabin for seeking to make peace with Palestinian leaders.

Over the centuries and certainly in our time, most Orthodox Jews have had good reason not to put these teachings into operation. Yet they remain part of classic Jewish instruction. After all, if God included such provisions in the Torah, it is not for human beings to countermand them. That is the theological basis for zealotry in all religions: We know what God wants us to do, and there is no authority in the universe that can give more compelling commands to desist from doing it. True, considering the awesome consequences, most Orthodox leaders will not want to take on the burden of such certainty of God's will, particularly when in even lesser matters there is often much debate about just what the halachic duty is. The zealot, however, doesn't want to be wishy-washy about serving God. In a way, he or she believes that non-activist fellow believers are worse than the non-Orthodox, for they know God's truth and yet don't or won't act on it.

This certainty of knowing what God wants of them separates more traditional Jews from their liberal kin. Our non-Orthodoxy arises just here, from our belief that human beings cannot know absolutely what God wants us to do. We believe that we humans are partners in whatever revelation exists; therefore, we know enough to try to discover what it is that God commands. Thus our knowledge of God's will is always bound by the human element. Our comparatively limited if compelling understanding of revelation is not found in the classic Jewish texts; this God-human partnership is liberal Judaism's contribution to Jewish belief.

The authors of the Bible and the Talmud were convinced that the people of Israel and no others can understand the one full, correct truth about God and human duty. Jewish liberals believe that no person's and no group's knowledge of God or claim to revelation is so certain that people should *ever* coerce others to believe and practice as they do. For us, fanaticism is a primal sin.

Liberals pay a religious price for their notion of participatory revelation. We cannot say with insistence regarding Passover or Shabbat observance that God wants us to do this or desist from doing that. It is always possible for liberal Jews to reply that, while we are grateful for guidance, we read God's will differently. The one area in which liberal Jews manifest a kind of tempered zeal is ethical urgency—what the German philosopher Immanuel Kant called the "categorical imperative," the unqualified necessity to do the good. In this area, non-Orthodox Jewish observance has been impressive.

Indeed, even liberals have had what may be called their own "ethical fanatics." They are that tiny minority who become so taken by one ethical issue or another that they cannot imagine other people thinking differently or having sensible questions about what is being asked of them. Our quasi-zealots may make real nuisances of themselves—the evocative Yiddish term for them is "nudnicks"—

but fortunately, they are most unlikely to resort to violence. While the behavior of these zealots says more about human nature than about their beliefs, at least it is evidence of how seriously many take their ethical obligations. It is, of course, stretching things quite a bit to compare nuisance zealots to the murderous fanatics we often see and hear about these days. Nonetheless, it is important to make my fellow liberal Jews aware that even the best of teachings cannot safeguard us from what the human heart perversely creates.

17

Who Is a *Mentsh?*

Gershom Scholem, the preeminent Jewish scholar of much of the twentieth century, rarely allowed himself to generalize without a massive amount of evidence to support him. It seems to me, however, that on one theme, Scholem allowed himself to speak as much from his Jewish heart as from his incomparable Jewish learning, namely: what our classic teachers considered ideal types of Jews. Scholem identified three: the sage (*talmid hacham*), the righteous (*tzaddik*), and the pious one (*hasid*). He identified the *talmid hacham* as the Jewish religion's intellectual ideal and the *hasid* as its emotional counterpart. Between them stood the ordinary Jew who fulfilled more commandments than committed sins, the *tzaddik*. Of course in reality, the types were not exclusive but largely blended; just think of the legends about Rabbi Akiba, who lived in the second century CE and was one of the greatest teachers of the Talmudic period.

Scholem's wonderful paper on this topic, "Three Types of Jewish Piety," prompted me to speculate on what modern Jewry might add to his list, and I did not have to ponder the matter for long. I think we all would agree that a good Jew must also be a *mentsh*, and I refuse to transliterate the Yiddish as *mensch*, a German word. For me, the German *mensch* is heavily freighted with what Americans would call "manhood" (opera buffs, please note how Sarastro, the High Priest in Mozart's "The Magic Flute," describes a *mensch*), but the inherited Yiddish *mentsh* is concerned more with humanity.

What, then, is involved in being a *mentsh*? As usual with such highly charged terms, no single definition will satisfy all of the Jewish relatives who like to throw in a Yiddish expression now and then, much less the academic Yiddishists or anthropologists of eastern European life. At its simplest level—and particularly when applied to the young, as in "Be a *mentsh*!"—the term has overtones of the English phrase "Grow up!" It reminds the young that there is an adult ideal they should try to reach, and that we are unlikely to tolerate certain kinds of childishness that, though cute now, won't be much longer. I hear that sense of the ideal in the old Yiddish adage, "Be a *mentsh* and you can sit in the sukkah [the outdoor hut in which the autumn holiday of Sukkot is celebrated]." Closely related is the term used as a descriptive of human nature, as in, "A *mentsh* is often made a fool of by his own nature," or more caustically, "What a *mentsh* does to himself, ten enemies wouldn't do to him." Or the term can be used for analytic purposes: "A *mentsh* has big eyes but doesn't see his own faults."

Often describing human weaknesses, such negative uses of *mentsh* are relatively developmental. These old Yiddish uses imply that there is a certain maturity a person should strive to attain. But as we have seen in the last few proverbs, the term can expand beyond simple description to provide a sense of the ideal. It is this optimal Jewish sense embedded in the term that gives *mentsh* its special relevance. *Mentsh* can be pungently negative, as in, "That's why God gave a person two ears but only one mouth, so that a person, a *mentsh*, should listen more and talk less." Or it can point to a standard beyond ordinary practice, as in the disappointment with a community in which no one wishes to take the lead in doing the right thing, "A big crowd but not a single *mentsh* in it." That critical tone, reminiscent of the prophets, echoes in these old usages: "There's little worse for a person than having another person over him"; "One should fear God but beware of people"; "God only punishes but people take revenge." This comes to a climax in the judgment, "That's something that shouldn't happen to any human being."

In more recent times—here I offer evidence from my youth—the term *mentsh* took on a special tone, perhaps one brought on by Jews' growing economic success. It had to do with the behavior of those who had, in one way or another, become successful, that is, had risen in social class, or attained prestige or power. In the customary order of things, that entitled them to be snooty, to indicate their increased status by not needing to be nice to ordinary folks. But if an individual continued to be considerate of others, we said that he was a real *mentsh*.

Today the term is often used as a commendation for those who are still aware and attentive to us lesser beings, whom they might easily ignore. Then we say of such a person, "She's a real *mentsh*." I suppose we could put that sentiment into English or Hebrew, but there is something about our *mameloshen,* our Yiddish "mother tongue," that not only says this but much, much more.

In sum, it seems to me that today's addition to the ideal adds the notion of simple humanity to the old Jewish image of the *tzaddik,* the righteous person that Gershom Scholem identified several decades ago. Of course we would still like our common ideal type to do more righteous deeds than sins. But in keeping with our extraordinary emergence into the world at large and the expanded possibilities that have opened for contemporary Jews, we want our ideal person to not only do good but to radiate goodness. In ways that our tradition could only occasionally glimpse, we want deeds to be accompanied by character, by an embracing decency, and by an unfailing sensitivity of soul. All of these human qualities are so intangible, they must be packed into the beloved Yiddishism *mentsh.*

III
Creating Sacred Community

18

A Mystical Model
for Leaders

If sex was another generation's "dirty little secret," as the novelist D. H. Lawrence stated, surely the most poorly kept confidence of our time would be power. Not only in the political arena but in venues from board room to bedroom, we engage each other in bareknuckle battles that would make champion prize fighters wince. Since our hope for accomplishment rests largely on how power is organized and dispensed, it is little wonder that our generation has chosen Donald Trump as the exemplar of power in action, as every would-be apprentice would agree. Yet what has moved many to despair is the realization that almost everywhere we look, we see power abused. So how might we transform even a benevolent tyrant into a responsible, responsive human being?

We can find a fresh model for contemporary leadership and simultaneously be au courant by exploring the brilliant kabbalistic speculations about God taught by Isaac Luria of Safed, the most creative Jewish mystic and teacher of the premodern period. This sixteenth-century mystic developed an astonishing doctrine of creation around three innovative concepts: *tzimtzum*, "contraction"; *sh'virah*, "smash up"; and *tikkun*, "restoration."

Creation is usually thought of in spatial terms and is envisioned as a movement of externalization, that is, God puts the Creation "out there." Think of Michelangelo's Sistine Chapel mural. Mighty, muscular God stretches God's full arm's length to one fingertip and brings Adam into being. Just so, for most of us, creation is normally an act of self-extension.

Luria felt otherwise. If God is everywhere, he reasoned, there's no "out there" in which to put the Creation! In order to create anything, God must first contract. God, said Luria, creates by pulling back, the act of *tzimtzum*. This act leaves a void that enables God's creatures to have a space in which to come into being.

As God withdraws, God leaves behind in the Creation-space a residue of God's reality, something like the small bit of oil that always is left even after we think we have emptied the jug. Typical of the incredible mix of metaphors in kabbalistic writing, the teachers speak of these also as remaining beams of God's creative light, producing vessels that fill with the light of Creation. But God's power proves too mighty for these vessels, and they shatter, the process Luria calls *sh'virah*. That's the problem with our world—we live among the shells or husks of what might have been. Yet some sparks of God's energizing light remain.

If every bit of God's divine sparks could mystically be restored to their proper place in God's being, all things would become as they were intended to be. Through human acts of *tikkun*, repair or restoration—what Luria understood as following the Torah in its full mystic depth—God's wholeness of creation would appear.

What astonishes us is Luria's bold insistence that *tikkun* is primarily the work of humanity, not the work of God. Luria has shifted the power to bring the Messiah from God's hands to ours! This human-centered action developed in the later idea of democracy, what we moderns know as a form of government in which leaders are duly chosen by a majority of their peers.

We can easily translate this vision into contemporary ethical terms. We regularly see leaders who misuse their power by operating through their own self-aggrandizement, minimally concerned with maintaining a humanizing effect on those they lead. The Lurianic model of leadership requires leaders to judiciously withhold presence (and power!) so their followers have the space they need to act on their own.

Consider the contrast between the older and newer clergy leadership models. In the older style, the clergy were so busy doing things *for* us that they left us little opportunity to try things by ourselves. They talked so much that when they stopped and asked for questions or honest comments, we often didn't really believe that they wanted to hear us. At their worst, they thought the only way to create was to fill the space with their self-importance. Compare this to the leadership styles of our younger clergy, who are taught to lead by wisely making room for others.

To be sure, the leader's contracting *tzimtzum* must always be followed by the sending of creative beams of light into the just-vacated void. Indeed, leadership in the Lurianic style is particularly difficult because it requires continuous flip-flopping. Now we hold back and now we act, while danger lurks equally in excess of either action or inaction. Premature or too frequent interventions in the classroom, for example, are as troublesome as missing caution signs that the students need some help. This same idea holds as true in a family discussion as it does in a task force or committee we may lead.

Were this problem not challenging enough, we must constantly be on guard, lest our decision to intervene merely screen a power grab; our decision to stay silent may signal a punishing withholding when sparks of creativity are truly necessary. Lurianic leadership depends on an exquisite sense of interpersonal rhythm. It also depends on a capacity to forgive both ourselves and others, those whose need for independence may frustrate our own plans. It isn't easy, but it's the only way to re-create the world in God's sacred image.

How an Agnostic Community Came to Seek Spirituality

19

Books celebrating the 350th anniversary of American Jewry in 2004 certainly are a tribute to the high standards of Jewish academic writing, and they seem to reflect their authors' understanding of what kind of history needs to be written these days. So it is as an admirer of their work that I want to comment on what I find missing from their depictions of late-twentieth-century developments in our community, the period of my own maturation as a rabbi and as a frequent writer and teacher of Jewish theology.

My interests have centered on what we today can believe, specifically the kinds of religious thinking that underlie our community's diverse Jewish practices. The historians, by contrast, are largely concerned with the social development of the past sixty years—the institutions that shaped so much of Jewish life in America, and the leaders and events that gave those decades their special Jewish tone. It seems to me their accounts neglected the critical spiritual shift and the simultaneous reconnection to personal religious faith that significantly occurred at this time.

I can make my point best by contrasting these challenges with respect to two related changes that took place in the years following World War II. One was a transition from a community with a passion for Americanizing (and therefore compulsively dedicated to de-ghettoizing), to a community relatively secure in its social integration and now concerned with affirming its Jewishness. Our historians covered this transition reasonably well. In contrast, the second religious change—from widespread agnosticism to the present significant openness to God—was almost totally ignored. I believe that what happened is worth comment, although I am not a historian but someone who lived through and participated in a religious transition whose effects are still substantially felt. My specifically religious interests seemed odd to my fellow rabbinical students in the 1940s; however, I was fortunate enough to find two friends at the Hebrew Union College, Arnold Jacob Wolf and Steven S. Schwarzschild, who felt the same way. After we were ordained in 1948, we found a few recent graduates of the Jewish Theological Seminary (the institution that ordains Conservative rabbis), who had similar views, and a wonderful German émigré to this continent, Emil Fackenheim. In our various ways, we all endeavored to make God a living reality in American Judaism.

We can best trace the changes we sought if we turn back to the 1920s and 1930s and take note of the antireligious mindset of the community's then-passion for Americanization. The immigrant Jewish piety of the time centered on practices that led Jews to keep socially separate from other Americans; despite the challenges of those days, they believed that massive change could only meaningfully arrive by the coming of the Messiah. Jews who were flocking to the university as a means of social advancement considered that belief in a personal God unscientific, and chose politics as the surest means of achieving social change. Not everyone became a card-carrying atheist, but while some still had a high regard for perpetuating Jewish life, few had any significant interest in Jewish belief.

By the time of the postwar boom of the late 1940s, to the early 1960s, confidence in science and rationality had radically lessened, and a suburban exodus replaced neighborhood Jewishness, accompanied by the need to affiliate with a synagogue for one's children to know they were Jews. Since America was now seen as the home of three great religions—Protestantism, Catholicism, and Judaism—atheism among us gave way to a general if quiet Jewish agnosticism. That is, people didn't bother arguing that there was no God; they often said they would believe in God if provided with acceptable proof that such a Being existed. As synagogue life burgeoned, the laity and much of the rabbinate were content to bracket the God-question while celebrating Jewish culture, fighting anti-Semitism, working for tolerance, and promoting Jewish ethics and its social-justice imperatives.

All this changed in the mid-1960s, when believing Protestants talked excitedly about "Death of God" theology at the same time that a shocking consciousness of the Holocaust became widespread among Jews. This unprecedented evil seemed to decide the Jewish rejection of God. By the early 1970s, a freshly empowered Jewish agnosticism freely proclaimed its intellectual superiority and grandly predicted that American Jewry had matured enough to face a Godless future.

Rarely has so widely ballyhooed an intellectual claim been so quickly rejected by the community. I recall rabbis in the early 1970s who were afraid that the new Humanistic Judaism would soon supersede the synagogue movements they were identified with. But within a few years, it began to be clear that while most Jews did not believe much, they did believe *something*; we actually began hearing of *chavurot* and New Age mystic groups forming. Already in the 1980s, American Jews were clearly headed away from humanism. By the 1990s, much of the community was involved in searching for Jewish spirituality (a euphemism for involvement with a God still kept at arm's length), Jewish mysticism (a promise of intimacy with God), or Kabbalah (an intimate detailing of God's ten interactive aspects).

What factors brought on these astonishing changes?

First, our view of human nature was changed in large measure as a result of the great evils that allegedly intelligent and apparently cultured human beings continually do. The Death of God movement had prided itself on fully enfranchising human responsibility by eliminating divine influence on human events. But as one national and social outrage followed another, as the scams and deceptions of our leaders multiplied (such as what the Pentagon Papers showed about the Vietnam War and the Watergate burglary cover-up), we began to doubt that looking to only ourselves as the source of our values could guide us to beneficent ends. So we became open to the possibility that Some Ultimate Source of value could direct us, if we could only pay attention to it.

Second, at the same time, the philosophical certainties that had grounded our old agnosticism collapsed. Once, philosophers like Immanuel Kant confidently said that being rational involved responding to a moral law that addressed us all. But this notion of pure reason mandating ethics died from a host of challenges: Marx said ethics came from socioeconomic interests; Freud pointed to our early emotional ties; anthropologist Margaret Mead claimed that normative behavior was culturally generated; people of color referred to mandated ethics as a tool of colonialism; and feminists charged they were a tool of male domination. Ethics' loss of a philosophically universal, demanding position continues to this day.

The combination of these practical and philosophic reversals has, I believe, led to the unanticipated yet vigorous American interest in various forms of spirituality. Among Jews, the move from an ethics so certain it could dispense with God—the old agnosticism—has now given way to a somewhat wary involvement with God as the ground of our values, what I would consider a growing openness to Jewish religiosity.

Let me put this personally. Some decades back, when people came to *shul,* I observed them mostly hoping that the liturgy would move briskly, the rabbi would say something thoughtful (preferably quickly), and, finding some friends, they'd pick up the latest gossip. Today, while all that is still important, people regularly want the mood and music to touch them. Not a few hope to find themselves here, as in few other places, in the Presence of God. We still find it difficult to speak of our religiosity, but as I have prayed, davened, in diverse synagogues, I have found this sensibility widespread.

And it is this extraordinary transformation in American Jewry that I did not find discussed in the recent histories of our community.

20

The Appeal of Transdenominational Judaism

The trendy talk about transdenominational (TD) Judaism and its fraternal twin, nondenominational (ND) Judaism, has stirred some dust in the archives I call my mind. I think I can recall three prior versions of the present discussion that may help clarify this phenomenon a little better.

The first was precipitated by some public relations efforts from a new ND rabbinical school that boasted it would be the first Jewish seminary to grant a TD *s'michah*, an ordination accepted by any Jewish congregation. I rarely seek to try to correct people who make Jewish mistakes while pleading their case to the media, but this time I did, and the school has since stopped making this claim. In fact, the first TD rabbinical school to be established and survive for a solid length of time was the Jewish Institute of Religion, founded by Stephen S. Wise in 1922. That noble experiment came to an end when it merged with the Hebrew Union College in 1950.

In the 1940s and 1950s, as the old postimmigrant neighborhoods broke up and Jews moved to the suburbs and increasingly set up and joined synagogues, the Reform and Conservative movements expanded greatly. Some congregations sought to remain free of affiliation and thus are evidence of a second ND phenomenon. Rather rare today they still maintain their independence, though their rabbis probably graduated from recognized denominational seminaries.

The third and most substantial nondenominational push came from the *havurah* movement, which began in the 1960s. These individual groups of Jews were moved by a do-it-yourself ethos to creatively explore and commemorate diverse facets of their faith, enhanced by a commitment to the smallness and informality that fostered person-to-person familiarity. A number of groups could rely on the expertise of rabbis or Jewish academics who belonged to a particular *havurah* and were not employed by a synagogue.

From what I can gather about the present interest in TD Judaism, it seems to be largely a big-city phenomenon—New York City's Upper West Side being the hotbed of this activity—and it appeals primarily to young adults, many with a solid Jewish education. I should think this development would make a wonderful research topic for some adventurous anthropologist looking for a new "tribe" to study, or for those sociologists who keep surveying our community, often to confront us with what is not going well with American Jews. Having no such data to go on, my comments are largely based on what I've read and discussions I've had with various people.

Though I am a lifetime employee of a Jewish denomination, Reform Judaism, I find much in transdenominationalism that all caring Jews might celebrate. Most people in our community are so busy enjoying the various seductions of North American consumerism that it's a special joy to hear about those—young people yet!—whose dissatisfaction with our religious practice has led them to want to be actively Jewish in their own distinctive way. In fact, they feel reasonably certain that they can comfortably manage its ritual requirements without professional aid. Thus they feel competent to do all that needs to be done at worship services—chanting prayers, reading Torah, giving a sermon. Apparently we did something right—in our schools and camps and travel experiences and university courses and all the rest of what we hoped would empower a critical mass of our young adults in their Jewishness.

Perhaps I am so optimistic about what they are doing because I personally have had so many positive encounters with what in effect have been intimations of TD Judaism. My father often recalled how in his youthful hometown community—Sokoly, in pre–World War I Russian Poland—people mostly went to small *shtieblach* (something like American storefront shuls) differentiated by the occupations of their founders, like the tailors' or the shoe-makers' *shtieblach*, and only gathered in the "big shul" on major hol-idays. Besides, in my case this attitude may be congenital. My great-grandfather would cross the street so as not to pass too close to a Hasid, because the Vilna Gaon, the leading Jewish legal authority of the late eighteenth century, put the movement in *herem* (the Jewish equivalent of Catholic "excommunication," fun-damentally a form of community ostracism). Yet his beloved Litvak grandson, my father, married (in America) the daughter of a Hasid.

Add to this my experience in the world of Jewish studies. In aca-demic journals, where the flow of Jewish scholarship is approaching flood stage, what you say about your topic has little or nothing to do with the Jews you feel most comfortable praying with, or for that matter, if you happen to be a Jewish secularist and pray seldom, if at all. What counts is the style of what we religious types privately call *talmud torah*, the study of Torah, how you have supported your con-tention with data and logically established your conclusions.

The most persuasive work I have ever read about the virtues of Jewish denominationalism was written by Milton Steinberg in his 1947 book, *Basic Judaism*. He argued that, from the standpoint of Jewish belief, we really ought to have only two varieties of Judaism, traditional and modern. What most seriously divides contemporary Jews is whether we accept the authority of the Oral Law, the Tal-mudic and ongoing rabbinic counterpart to the Written Law, the first five books of the Bible, known as the Torah. Or do we modify

Judaism in terms of what the university has taught about the historical development of human affairs?

Particularly in light of the large overlap between Conservative, Reconstructionist, and Reform Judaism, I have always believed Steinberg to be theoretically correct. Practically, however, Jews have found it congenial to create more than his two types of Jewish religious streams. If anything, Orthodox Jews are more splintered and independent than are non-Orthodox Jews. There are many interpretations that define what proper observance of Jewish law entails, and no central organization to unify the various groups. Moreover, when it comes to creating major institutions—summer camps, seminaries with full-time academics and first-rate libraries that train rabbis and cantors and educators to bring their best skills to our congregations, organizations that foster broad community support for major human and Jewish initiatives—small groups need what only large groups can provide. Besides, with most Americans complaining they are overworked and overscheduled, it is difficult to believe that they can also shoulder the many responsibilities required by do-it-yourself religious communal life.

With all that being said, I believe that those of us who prefer denominational life should encourage those who prefer smaller, more involving venues. Who knows what they may yet teach the rest of us about being better Jews?

21

A Conflict over
Interfaith Dialogue

Since 1993, when Rabbi Joseph Baer Soloveitchik died, no one has arisen to take his place as the intellectual and legal, or halachic, leader of what used to be called modern Orthodoxy, the piety that sought to embrace modern learning while observing traditional Judaism. Already recognized in his youth as a genius in halachic literature, he also earned a PhD in philosophy from the University of Berlin. In 1966 I had the privilege of writing the first academic analysis in English of his religious thought.

The Rav, as his many disciples reverently called him, exerted exceptional influence and held great prestige in the Orthodox rabbinate. Therefore he was often privately approached in the hope he would at least tacitly approve the Catholic statement *Nostra Aetate*, a document-in-the-making of the Second Vatican Council that presented a revolutionary, highly positive attitude toward the Jews and Judaism. Instead, in 1964 Soloveitchik published an essay titled "Confrontation" in the Orthodox Rabbinical Council's journal *Tradition*, some months before *Nostra Aetate* was released. This remains the basis for the Orthodox rejection of interfaith religious discussion.

In this article, the Rav explains why Jews should not participate in theological exchanges with other faiths: "We are, therefore, opposed to any public debate, dialogue or symposium concerning the doctrinal, dogmatic or ritual aspects of our faith vis-à-vis 'similar' aspects of another faith community." He goes on to give ten specific examples of topics it would be "improper to enter dialogues on," saying: "There cannot be mutual understanding concerning these topics, *for Jew and Christian will employ different categories and move within incommensurate frames of reference and evaluation*" (his emphasis). The statement concludes with a highly positive view of discussions dealing with "the public world of humanitarian and cultural endeavors. We are ready to discuss universal religious problems. We will resist any attempt to debate our private individual commitment." Though this article was written more than forty years ago, I believe it reflects the continuing thought and practice of today's centrist Orthodox Jewish rabbinate and therefore demands attention.

Rabbi Soloveitchik's argument for his position develops along two lines, one dealing with his anticipation of how such discussions might be conducted, and the other stemming from his understanding of the nature of religious faith.

In considering his first line of thought, it is instructive to cite his language about theological exchanges. He rejected any attempt to "engage us [Jews] in a peculiar encounter in which our confronter will command us to take a position beneath him while placing himself not alongside of but above us." Again, he opposed any meeting "in which we shall become an object of observation, judgment, and evaluation." And again, "Our singular commitment to God and our hope and indomitable will for survival are non-negotiable and non-rationalizable and are not subject to debate and argumentation." One wonders what Soloveitchik would make of the several decades of interfaith discussions since *Nostra Aetate*, with their record of respect and high regard. Moreover, he seems to have believed that the goal of such discussions is to reach mutual agreement, that is, that the purpose of interfaith dialogue is to attain a kind of fusion of faiths. However, Jewish-Catholic discussions have in fact increasingly focused on understanding each other's differences.

To be sure, it is important initially to identify areas of similarities, creating a foundation that makes communication possible. In the case of Judaism and Christianity, that foundation originates from our mutual dependence on the Hebrew Scriptures. It seems to me that because of this, Judaism and Christianity have a closeness that no other world religions share, a judgment that I cautiously assert without having greater clarity about Islam's general attitude regarding Hebrew Scriptures. Whatever the case, recent dialogue has indicated nothing like the indignities rightly rejected by the Rav.

His other argument against dialogue, that it violates the privacy of individual faith, demands a more subtle consideration. He summarized his argument as follows: "The great encounter between God and man is a wholly personal private affair incomprehensible to the outsider—even to a brother of the same faith community." He explained that encounter in several ways, such as: "It defies all standardized media of information and all objective categories," and "One of the confronters will be impelled to avail himself of the language of his opponent ... [leading to a] surrender of individuality and distinctiveness."

One hears in Soloveitchik's stance an echo of Psalm 65:2, *L'cha dumiyah t'hillah*, which may be read simply as "Praise befits You." A midrash endearingly turns this into "To You silence is praise," for what might a human ever say that would be adequate to God's reality? Jews echo this sentiment regularly in the Kaddish, the prayer of praise for God that frames parts of our liturgy and is best known for being recited by mourners at the conclusion of most worship services.

True, we cannot fully communicate to someone else the grounding experiences of our faith. Yet does that mean we can say nothing useful about those experiences? I do not think it mere pedantry to point out that Soloveitchik himself usefully communicated a good deal about intimate religious experience. Moreover, I believe that to say what one *can* say, even when one cannot adequately say all that one *would like* to say, makes it possible for faiths that have long been estranged to become less alien to one another. Having enlightened hints as to what moves our neighbors not only gives us a richer sense of who they are and what we may reasonably expect of them, it does so in a way that honors their individuality and invites reciprocal respect.

Let me press forward with this counterargument in favor of saying the sayable by recounting a personal experience. For its meeting in the late 1970s, the American Theological Society decided to discuss contemporary Christologies, the traditional and innovative interpretations of Jesus as the son of the one God. I, a member for a number of years of this by-invitation-only association, was invited to present what a believing Jew could say about these several interpretations of the central Christian mystery.

At this advanced level of theological discussion, two difficulties quickly presented themselves to me, in addition to the problem of intimacy that Rabbi Soloveitchik had identified. The first difficulty came from the fact that like all other thinking, the ways in which people explain and justify religious belief change with time. Since my graduate school study of Christian theology two decades earlier, new ways of thinking about Christology had emerged. The second difficulty was that there wasn't just one Christology to consider, but a rich pluralism of views in both Protestant and Roman Catholic thought. These problems of change and variety were not insurmountable. At my request, my Christian colleagues provided me with a bibliography of works they believed fairly spanned the current significant views of Christology. The rest was up to me.

True, I could only follow the Christian arguments part of the way—sometimes more, sometimes less. But the exercise certainly was not in vain. I realized that if Christian thinkers had been studying what contemporary Jewish thinkers say about Torah or Covenant, they would have had a similar experience.

This kind of serious theological discussion revealed a nearness in our differences, which clearly has brought me closer to my Christian colleagues. At the same time, the conversations clarified what would continue to divide us. Contrary to Rabbi Soloveitchik's argument, this encounter has been repeated over the ensuing decades, much to my satisfaction. Being able to participate in sacred dialogue with my friends of many religious persuasions has helped me to better understand and affirm my own beliefs, for which I will always be grateful.

22

How Liberal and Orthodox Jews Can Coexist

Orthodox spokesmen often propose a simple solution to the ongoing problem of achieving Jewish unity. They suggest that since liberal, non-Orthodox Jews have adapted to so much in today's world, we should agree to accept the life prescribed by Torah, the halachah, in matters particularly critical to them, those related to Jewish identity. The rules regarding keeping kosher (*kashrut*) provide a good example: "You can eat in my house, but I can't eat in yours. Why don't you agree to follow my practice?"

In my experience, thoughtful traditionalists may not understand that liberal Jews frequently put aside classic Jewish law because of their religious principles. The first task, then, is to show that what others may perceive as a rejection of Judaism arises from a heartfelt commitment to Jewish belief and devotion. The critical issue becomes how liberal Jews have reshaped their Jewish duty to the One God.

Non-Orthodox Jews mostly agree that a knowledgeable conscience helps determine Jewish obligations. When human welfare is involved, people must hear a command that demands our attention and action. We Jews know from overcoming our own suffering through the ages that sanctifying human relations is our primary responsibility; it continues to guide and inspire us in our lives of Jewish prayer, ritual, and study. Each individual's unique capacity for religious experience has to begin with a heightened concern for humanity.

Frankly, I think that only a Judaism that respects conscientious individual decisions can flourish today. For me, this is not merely a pragmatic consideration but a faith I find implicit in the Torah's teaching, which says that we are "created in the image of God."

I must admit that liberals like me should be more careful about two things that indicate how our commitments obligate us, even as halachah does for Orthodox Jews. First, other Jews would take us more seriously if our pious elite were greater numerically and their activity more visible. Second, other Jews would better understand the depth of our religiosity if, instead of regularly talking about human feelings or needs, we would speak of what God wants of us. We do not speak of God and obligation differently than other Jews do. We, too, assert that our duties come from our sense of how God wants us to live the Covenant today. If we are understood in these terms, few other Jews would ask us to deny our sense of God and Torah for the sake of a more united Jewish community.

That being said, we must face a harsh reality. If conscience is to be respected, we cannot ask the Orthodox to violate their faith and accept liberal Judaism as a fully equivalent interpretation of Judaism. The basic, authoritative texts of Jewish law clearly classify our modernist reinterpretation of Judaism as heretical. Ideally, it can never be condoned. On both sides, then, the protagonists stand on principle, and these stands are irreconcilable.

Despite all these intractabilities, both sides have identified a way that might help to overcome the present impasse: a commitment to the love for the Jewish people and individual Jews (*Ahavat Yisrael*). One of the many things Jews have learned from living in democracies is that a lot of good can come from learning to live and work with people whose beliefs and customs we may disagree with. While certainly there are limits to such cooperation, the Jewish community has been able to achieve considerable consensus on some issues.

Pragmatically, although neither group lacks power, neither is strong enough to force the other to do its will. While in recent years Orthodoxy has been growing, it still appeals to only a small minority of American Jews. Liberal Judaism speaks to the unarticulated faith of most contemporary Jews, sanctifying what they hold most precious: gender equality and acceptance, the dignity of each person, and the virtue of understanding that their generation's social arrangements may be changed by those who come after them. With neither group able to enforce its views on the other, levelheadedness may lead both Orthodox and liberal Jews to permit their love of Judaism to aid them in their search for a mutually acceptable accommodation. Believing Jews—here liberal and Orthodox Jews stand as one—will seek the good of the Jewish people as a whole, not in some low-though-common denominator, but in terms of what we all believe God desires us to do.

I do not see that the substance of any possible understanding with the Orthodox can be worked out in public. Even in private, neither side will negotiate matters of fundamental principle. What we need today are leaders who show their moral courage and political sagacity, creating out of what *can* be done a faithful reflection of what *ought* to be done.

Might we consider that the burdens our leaders carry may differ only in degree from what each of us shoulders individually in his or her life? God obligates us all to be holy not in some general, abstractly spiritual way but in the humdrum particularities of making and spending money, of working with some against the designs of others, of loving and hating and being indifferent, of the situations we are stuck with as well as those we can create to our will.

My Judaism seeks to make me a realist who is not cynical, an idealist who is not naive. My Judaism calls on me to practice the higher politics, the lofty art of living Torah.

The Special Risk of Liberalizing Judaism

23

I recently read an article about Rabbi Jonathan Sacks, Great Britain's chief rabbi, that praised him for his positive, flexible view toward contemporary Orthodoxy's interpretation of Jewish law. I can imagine the empathy my fellow liberal rabbis must have felt for Rabbi Sacks's position. Nonetheless, I think such enthusiasm is largely misplaced and, with all my appreciation for his view of Orthodoxy, I'd like to explain why.

Let me begin by identifying the challenge that faces both Orthodox and non-Orthodox Jews and causes us to worry about the proper mix of continuity and change in current Jewish practice. A historical note may help. Although this may seem counterintuitive, I want to argue that in the early to mid-nineteenth century, *first* the various liberal Judaisms came into being and only *then*, in response, did Orthodoxy emerge. Of course, traditional Judaism goes back a couple of thousand years, to the beginnings of rabbinic Judaism. But when scholars today speak of the appearance of Orthodoxy only one and a half centuries back, they have a quite specific development in mind. They are focusing on how some leaders of traditional Judaism sought to counter the new liberal interpretations of Judaism and its advocacy of substantial modification to the old patterns of Jewish observance.

The liberals did this by creating an explicitly activist interpretation of what had long been the implicitly classic, conservative Jewish attitude toward continuity and change. While in prior generations, Jews had lived their religious lives without needing abstract criteria by which to validate or reject innovations, now, in reaction to the liberals' unprecedented innovations, a modern ideology of traditional Judaism—Orthodox Judaism—arose that sought to do precisely that.

The communal crisis of those tumultuous days centered on the extent of changes in Jewish practice in response to the fundamental alteration in the social status of Jews in western Europe. As Jews were increasingly accepted as near-equals in society—one substantially permeated with Christian values, to be sure—they eagerly sought to take advantage of the economic, intellectual, and personal opportunities newly opened to them. But Jewish law, fashioned over the centuries in response to the outsider status of Jews, largely sought to reinforce Jewish distinctiveness. The inward orientation made the prescribed way of life, halachah, relatively inhospitable to modernizers' call for worship and preaching in the vernacular, education primarily in secular rather than religious areas, and less isolating patterns for eating and Sabbath observance.

I certainly do not mean to suggest that classic Jewish law had no capacity for change and innovation. Both Hanukkah and Simchat Torah (the celebration of concluding and then beginning again the reading of the Torah), for example, are Jewish holidays unknown to biblical Judaism but mandatory for the Rabbis. Today, despite the deep-seated Jewish aversion to pigs, the current widespread medical use of pig heart valves to replace defective human ones is accepted by Orthodox legal authorities. To give another example, while there is substantial difference among authorities, many Orthodox rabbis have accepted brain death and the consequent harvesting of organs for transplant.

So I think that there are good historical reasons for Rabbi Sacks to make his case for Orthodoxy's flexibility. However, I see two other factors that may have influenced him. The first is that his community, mainline British Orthodoxy, historically has been hospitable to a broad but not radical range of interpretation and practice. The second is that some of the changes liberals once called for and were fought by the traditional rabbinate have proved their worth over the years, perhaps most notably in the use of the vernacular in teaching classic Jewish texts. This is indicated by the unprecedented popularity of the Schottenstein translation of the Talmud.

But what liberal rabbis most likely have in mind when they speak of the "flexibility" required of Judaism in our time is quite different from Rabbi Sacks's limited appreciation of innovation in the law. It surely was not halachic flexibility that the leading traditional rabbis demonstrated when they opposed the substantial changes that modernizing Jewry required for their postghetto existence. Indeed, it was this relatively traditionalist inflexibility that prompted courageous laypeople to take matters into their own hands and create what became the several forms of non-Orthodoxy.

These pioneers believed that Judaism had to be saved from what was seen as religious stagnation in the face of the unprecedented social upheaval created by the Jews' no longer being Europe's perennial outsiders. Those promoting transformation were certain that Judaism could, in these special circumstances, tolerate—perhaps even mandate—radical change. These Jews made a "wager" that non-Orthodox Jews are still living out. They simply went ahead and created synagogues adapted to modern standards, with less repetitious services, more group decorum and prayers and preaching in the vernacular. In the process they gave up the classic theory of God's revelation of the Written and the Oral Laws and the Jewish inviolability of the halachah. That is, they gave up the belief, first mentioned in the Talmud, that at Mt. Sinai, God had also revealed instructions called the Oral Law, those not written on tablets, as well as the Written Law. This Oral Law authorized future rabbinic scholars to modify, extend, or even innovate what Jews must do. And that belief continues to this day. However, as Jews entered the modern world in increasing numbers, they overwhelmingly abandoned the notion of the Oral Law's eternal authority.

While Rabbi Sacks did not say so, let me say for him and all of us that no one should underestimate how very risky repudiating the authority of rabbinic Oral Law was and continues to be. In the name of saving Judaism, we may have gravely weakened it and changed its fundamental character. Of course, I am convinced that there were and still are good reasons for our radicalism, and I have written much to explain and defend our daring. But whether future Jewish historians will one day judge us as daring saviors of Judaism or as slow assimilationists I cannot unambiguously say.

Since I was ordained in 1948, I have seen many positive changes in non-Orthodox theory and practice that have given me great hope for our future. But I see no way that the leaders of Orthodoxy, even ones as admirable as Rabbi Sacks, can accept a kind of Jewish pluralism in which our views of Sabbath observance, women's rights in Judaism, and patrilineal descent of Jewish identity can easily be recognized as Torah. We have made our spiritual wager, and now we must wait for God and Jewish generations to come to judge whether we were wise in doing so.

Catholic–Jewish Dialogue: An Autobiographical Note

24

O ne of the benefits of getting older is the special perspective the years may provide, which holds true not just for significant moments but for those events which turn out to be utterly unanticipated. This has been particularly real in my life with regard to the dramatic changes in Catholic-Jewish relationships. My sense of that development has been powerfully shaped by personal experience.

In the beginning of 1965 I was fortunate to be invited to attend what I believe was the first formal Jewish-Catholic conference held in the United States, taking place at the oldest Benedictine monastery in America, St. Vincent's Archabbey in Latrobe, Pennsylvania. *Nostra Aetate*, the Second Vatican Council's pathbreaking declaration on the relationship between the Church and Judaism, denouncing anti-Semitism and affirming God's Covenant with the Jews, had not yet been promulgated. But there was so clear a sense of something significant happening to the Church's official attitude toward Judaism that the American Benedictine Academy sponsored that January meeting, which was attended by thirteen representatives of each faith.

I vividly remember my sense of trepidation. Traveling to St. Vincent's, I could not shake the fearfulness engendered by my Ohio childhood, and my memories of Catholic hostility and intransigence. That fear was expanded by what I had later learned of the Church's efforts over the centuries to convert or persecute Jews. I mention these fears because I believe that negative Jewish reaction to Catholicism may continue more often from the memories of these old traumas than from an attitude or action of contemporary Christians. These fears were compounded exponentially by the Holocaust, which heightened Jewish concern over even the remote possibility of losing another Jewish soul.

From all that I learned at Latrobe, two experiences still deeply affect me. First, I discovered that there were Catholics who, because of a new sensibility moving through their church, could speak to Jews and listen to them with simple human respect. Today this seems very modest, but to the thirteen Jews at St. Vincent's in 1965, it was a revolutionary discovery. Those days of study and encounter banished the specters of Christian denigration and proselytization from my fearful Jewish mind, enabling me to see the real human beings in front of me. In the ensuing decades, that understanding has been repeated many times in my encounters with Catholics.

The second experience concerned one Catholic present at the Latrobe meeting whom I already knew slightly. He was Phil Scharper, a former associate editor of the liberal lay-Catholic journal *Commonweal* and at the time an editor at Sheed and Ward publishers. As I recall, the start of our colloquy on the second day was delayed because it was a saint's feast day. A morning Mass would last longer than our program had allowed for, and members of the Jewish delegation were invited to attend. Although this was not the first Mass I had attended, it was an extraordinary experience to sit in the church as monks filled that great space with their beautiful music and chants. But I must confess that, as glorious as that experience was, it moved me only as an appreciative observer. Phil, seated to my right during the service, was devoutly praying the Mass, and his piety touched me to the depths of my soul.

I knew then and know now that he was praying to the God to whom I, too, prayed, that his devotion was directed to *Adonai,* my God and the God of my people. Phil's prayer echoed my own prayers in many ways. At a very elemental level, something at that moment changed my attitude toward Catholicism.

Fast-forward now to a relatively recent meeting devoted to what the decades of living with *Nostra Aetate* had taught both Catholics and Jews. Unlike the tentativeness and sensitivities so evident at Latrobe, this was a gathering of people long accustomed to speaking with one another from a rich knowledge of the two traditions. The very delegations present exemplified that. The Catholic group was headed by the cardinal who was the president of the Commission of the Holy See for Religious Relations with the Jewish People and he gave one of the major presentations of the evening. He, of course, could speak authoritatively for his church, which he did most elo-quently and thoughtfully.

By contrast, because Judaism has a totally different institutional form, with no built-in hierarchy or central agency, the Jewish pre-sentation was given by an individual scholar who, in effect, spoke for himself—namely, yours truly. Indeed, to remind my Christian listeners that the Jewish way of developing religious teaching was so different from theirs, I indicated that the other Jewish thinkers in the room might disagree with my ideas, and in that very divergence of views we would be faithfully creating Torah. Otherwise, I felt sure that the Catholic clergy and academics would be sufficiently sophis-ticated about Judaism to appreciate my words.

One other major theme of the evening has long stayed with me. Of course there was great good will manifested during the (kosher) dinner that preceded the addresses. This mood was strongly ampli-fied by the special mix of self-respect and respect for the other that permeated both speeches. Each speaker not only affirmed the worth of the other faith but did so in a manner that validated his own faith and at the same time indicated its differences with the other. Prior to the conference, no one had suggested that my presentation take this stance. Rather, the maturation of our relationship over the years made it seem natural for us not to hold back on the differences between us, when these were relevant to what we wanted to say.

Memories of the young man who went so fearfully to Latrobe many years before made this later evening particularly meaningful to me. Thus I took it upon myself to extend the blessing Jewish tradition prescribes when one sees a non-Jewish scholar of secular wisdom, and pronounced it over the Catholic teachers assembled before me: Blessed are You, *Adonai* our God, Sovereign of the universe, who has given of Your wisdom to flesh and blood. *Baruch atah Adonai, eloheinu melech haolam, shenatan mechochmato levasar vadam.*

The years since that event have confirmed my judgment in doing so.

25

The Historical Case for Interfaith Dialogue

Thank goodness, most of us native readers of English have grown up in societies where tolerance is the accepted norm—though life has been punctuated by enough acts of bigotry to force legislatures to pass hate-crime laws against them. So, we have little sense of what it must have been like to live when hatred for outsiders was the norm. Every once in a while, then, it helps to try to gain a sense of the prejudice that we Jews have faced for most of our history, in order to understand why most Jews today believe it is important to promote interfaith dialogue.

We have just about no records of what the nations who worshipped idols thought of our odd people, whose God was invisible and yet who stubbornly insisted that our Missing One was the one true God of the universe. By Roman times, we have a written sense of how peculiar and uncivilized our nation was considered, since it refused to work one day out of seven and rejected the oil ration given to the poor until the ration was certified ritually acceptable. Jews were so intolerant of other peoples' customs that when Roman legions came into Jerusalem with idolatrous animals pictured on their standards, a near-revolution broke out! So it is important to remember that there was considerable anti-Jewish sentiment way before Christians began accusing Jews of being responsible for Jesus' crucifixion or, in more bigoted theological language, of "killing God."

Then something completely unforeseen occurred. Christianity, which had started out as a Jewish sect, became an unprecedented success at proselytizing for its independently framed religiosity. In 380 CE, Emperor Theodosius proclaimed it to be the official religion of the Roman Empire.

With the rise of Christendom—a time when the Western Church was as much a political as a religious entity—we may imaginatively identify three periods of Jewish hatred. Until 1096, when the First Crusade began, Jews in Europe were social outcasts but were only occasionally physically attacked. Once the crusaders decided to punish Jews they encountered along the way to the Holy Land, Jewish existence became more hazardous. The rising intolerance took a special turn in the West around 1500, when the Italians began to establish ghettos and put other restrictions on their Jews. These were matched roughly by shtetls, the small Jewish villages of eastern Europe, and mellahs, the Jewish neighborhoods of North African communities in Muslim countries.

This bird's-eye view of a large chunk of Jewish history was more or less true until the French Revolution in 1789. Revolutionary France broke new ground by declaring after considerable debate that Jews were free and equal citizens of the new nation-state. And so we come to the modern period.

I take for granted that today, thoughtful Christians are ashamed of the ways in which their doctrines and institutions promoted the persecution of Jews. The memory of that history of violence and oppression is the activating force for the odd mix of euphoria and apprehension with which Jews embraced modernity and their legal and social acceptance. That apprehension was validated by the emergence of secular anti-Semitism in the nineteenth century and most virulently expressed by Nazism in the twentieth.

With the birth of modernity and its promise of equality, interfaith dialogue became theoretically possible; unfortunately this notion would not be fulfilled until the different faiths could speak together as equals, which did not occur for nearly another 150 years. Consider the experience of Moses Mendelssohn, the late-eighteenth-century figure often seen as the forerunner of all Jews who later made their way from the ghetto into modern culture. An internationally known and respected writer on culture and the human condition, he was challenged by a Christian minister, who asked why, with Mendelssohn's modern sensibilities, he did not give up his old, outmoded Jewish faith and become a Christian. Though always eager to avoid controversy, Mendelssohn had no choice but to reply. In 1783 he published a pathbreaking work entitled *Jerusalem*. Not surprisingly, it is mostly a plea for religious tolerance. It also includes an explanation of what constituted Jewish religious belief and why this strange minority faith called Judaism might appeal to a fully modern person. At this stage, "interfaith dialogue" may be said to have moved a step beyond medieval argument to polite antagonism.

Books such as Mendelssohn's *Jerusalem* continued to appear over the next century, but they never had a wide readership. The maturation of American democracy changed things. Streams of immigrants propelled a unique experiment in nation building, one grounded in the conviction that people of quite different points of view could live together to their mutual benefit.

Yet even here, prejudice and parochialism only slowly gave way to toleration. Not until after World War I did the first formal discussions among leaders of diverse religious groups seem to take on importance as a measure to increase the common welfare. And it wasn't until well after World War II that these small efforts expanded to include the idea that people could deepen their understanding of their own faith by being open to the teachings of the faiths of others.

Although originally beginning with a few open-minded members of the clergy who joined to speak publicly of their commonalities and differences, interfaith dialogue has now become accepted between teachers of various faiths and, in both academia and among lay people, between students of various religions.

For a people like the Jews, whose collective unconscious still vibrates with memories of more than a millennium of treatment as social pariahs, and whose recent history shows what can happen when a government does not respect difference, these develop-ments created a messianic hopefulness. Today this seems clear to most Jews: The vitality of their faith and the growth of American tolerance demands ongoing discussion and contact with representa-tives of every believing community in our society.

A messianic imperative is at work in all this. While it would be folly to expect its imminent fulfillment, it would be grievously sin-ful for us not to do our part in moving toward the repair and renewal of our world.

26

Building a Community of "God-Fearers"

There are no Jews in the first eleven chapters of the Bible. Instead, the old Hebrew creation stories discuss how God brought our universe into being, filled it with planets and seas and gave it all sorts of growing things—some fixed in place, others that roamed around. God then brought people into the universe, and, in contrast to God's other creations, God actually conversed with them. However, it turned out that the people had the unique "gift" of talking back to God, specifically by saying they refused to do what God wanted. As people multiplied, they kept doing evil; God, the stories say, finally got fed up. So God sent a flood to wipe out humankind except for one righteous man named Noah, his family, and a sampling of all the earth's animals.

After the Flood, God made a pact with Noah and his descendants, that is, all future humankind. God promised never again to send such destruction, put the rainbow in the sky as a reminder, and swore to keep the natural order pretty much as it had been. God renewed the charge made originally to Adam to have progeny and required certain new things of Noah and his family, specifically, that they not kill other people or eat the blood of animals they butchered.

These tales are filled with endless possibilities for comment; that's why almost everybody loves the Book of Genesis. Two things here particularly impress me. First, God is understood to care about all human beings. (Remember, there still aren't any Jews.) Second, by making this the first part of the Jews' saga, the old Hebrew sages who concocted it were insisting that you can't understand their people unless you first think in terms of God's relation with all humankind.

Much later, the Rabbis of the Talmud not only reaffirm but expand this teaching. God, they taught, has a continuing Covenant with humankind (the children of Noah or the Noahides) and gave them seven commandments they must follow: no idolatry, no blaspheming God, no stealing, no adultery, no murder, no cutting limbs from living animals, and the sole positive commandment, establishing just courts. The Rabbis debated whether a righteous gentile—one who fulfilled these commandments—had a share in the world to come. Later generations affirmed the positive view as a fixed part of Jewish law. All later Jewish theologies of the non-Jew begin with this tradition.

Sadly, historical circumstances long made it impractical for Jews to give this universalistic, broad agenda much attention. During the many centuries of Jewish subjugation, the primary Jewish religious obligation under the Covenant was to ensure our survival until God's sovereignty was fully established on earth. Even today, responsible Jewish leaders emphasize the importance of bolstering the health and safety of our own people. A significant number of Jews still believe that survival is so important and difficult a task that we must minimize our dialogue and connection with the greater community. They state that we ought to serve God by concentrating our energies on preserving our particular kin.

However, the overwhelming majority of American Jews believes that our country's unique espousal of tolerance—from which Jews have so wonderfully benefited—has given us an extraordinary opportunity to expand our religious horizon. While not neglecting our primary responsibility of strengthening the Jewish community, we can now take up our messianic task of seeking out the faithful Noahides and working with them to make God's name one on earth.

We can easily find echoes of this dedication in the Bible, with its frequent use of the phrase, "those that fear *Adonai*," recalling the Noahides or righteous gentiles. Sometimes the context makes plain that this is another term for "being religious," and refers to anything a good Hebrew should do. Scholars debate the meaning of "those who fear *Adonai*" when used in a broader context, such as in Psalm 118:1–4, which begins, "Praise *Adonai* for God is good, for God's lovingkindness is eternal." Then three verses follow, calling on different groups to offer such praise. The first group, in verse 2, is Israel, which one would assume is the whole Jewish people. The second group in verse 3 is the house of Aaron, the priests who have a special role in the Israelite praise of God. Then suddenly, in verse 4, where we might have expected something like "all the children of Jacob," or "all the house of Israel," we instead hear a call to "those who fear *Adonai*." That might mean all believing Hebrews, yet not only the inclusive language but the fact that all Jews were already included in verse 1 suggests that the poet is reaching out to any human being who believes in the God of the Jews.

There are a good number of such universalistic verses elsewhere in the Bible. Add similar statements from other parts of the Jewish tradition, and it seems reasonably clear that our sacred texts provide good reasons to participate in interfaith dialogue. In doing so, we are doing our part to fulfill the prayer with which we Jews have ended our services for well over a millennium.

> We … hope in You, *Adonai*, our God, that we may speedily see the glory of Your might: when You remove idols from the earth and cut off all false gods, perfecting the universe as God's own Dominion, when all flesh will call upon Your name and all the wicked of the earth turn to You, with all the denizens of earth recognizing and

knowing that every knee should bow to You and every tongue swear fealty. Before You they will bend the knee and prostrate themselves, rendering homage to Your glorious name, accepting upon themselves the yoke of Your Dominion that You may reign over them speedily and forever. For the Dominion is Yours and You will reign in glory for all eternity, as it is written in the Torah, "*Adonai* will reign for all eternity." And [as the prophet] said, "And *Adonai* will rule over all the earth. On that day, *Adonai* will be one and *Adonai*'s name will be one."

Ken yehi ratzon, may this speedily be God's will.

IV
Reading Sacred Texts

Letting the Psalms Speak to You

27

W hat aspects of the Jewish tradition—in addition to theology, which is admittedly abstract, indeed often abstruse—intrigue me? I love listening to fine liturgical music of all types and find that participating in worship usually gives me a sense of God's immediate presence, as well as a feeling of tranquility and well-being. Text study also brings me great satisfaction, but the surefire way to bring myself out of a funk is to spend some time with the Psalms. I simply love this biblical work, and I'm surprised that many people don't know about these magnificent 150 poems.

The Psalms speak to what is deeply personal in my faith, so those that deal with belief and its challenges especially touch me. Please keep in mind that I have no special expertise in this literature. I'm not a biblical scholar and I have not studied ancient Near Eastern mythology. But the glory of the Psalms is their universal accessibility; you don't need to be a professor to read and love them. Much of the poetry sounds as if it were written by ordinary people and thus is understood by ordinary people. That surely is why the Book of Psalms is, I believe, the only book of the Bible that is often published separately. People all over the world, despite their varied circumstances, have found its poetry meaningful. These often breathtakingly beautiful poems build on layers and layers of meanings and moods. What is happening in your life can often find expression in these words, written so long ago.

Take, for example, Psalm 8:

> *Adonai,* our Lord,
> How majestic is Your name throughout the earth …
> When I behold Your heavens, the work of Your fingers,
> The moon and the stars that You set in place,
> What is man that You have been mindful of him,
> Mortal man that You have taken note of him,
> That you have made him little less than divine,
> And adorned him with glory and majesty.
>
> (Psalm 8:2, 4–6)

This is a poem of awe. Someone goes outside, apparently at night, or remembers what it's like to go out at night, since the moon and stars are mentioned. And suddenly the poet realizes without benefit of telescope or any other instrument just how vast a universe it is. Overcome by this emotion, the psalmist has an appreciation of what it must have been like for our world to be brought into being. The poet's awe is twofold. The first part focuses on the Creator who made it. That is soon accompanied by the self-consciousness of what it means to be an appreciative human being, someone who has been given the power to respond to our vast universe and its Designer.

Gosh! That is about all that I, obviously no poet, can say. But although I'm not very poetic, at least I can be filled with wonder. Sadly, there are some who only want to "use" the sky—measure it, visit it, explore it, or even exploit it. Surely there is a place for that. But a religious person, a spiritual person, will more likely respond with a sense of "Wow!" that goes beyond language. The poet has given us words for our amazement at what God has done.

Although the psalmist starts with an extraordinary appreciation of God, this doesn't diminish the poet's appreciation of what it means to be a person. In fact, the author of Psalm 8 is equally awestruck by what it means to be part of the natural order, an animal like other animals and yet one that has been given the power to appreciate everything visible. Our poet also thrills at the insight that our unique ability to feel is but a small portion of God's special gifts to human beings. Indeed, every breath, every step, every taste, every smell, every joy are God's gifts to us. And the psalmist is simultaneously aware that all this abundance is connected to an intense, almost limitless sense of responsibility.

A second biblical poem, Psalm 27, does not conclude with such certainty of well-being:

> *Adonai* is my light and my help;
> whom should I fear?
> *Adonai* is the stronghold of my life,
> whom should I dread?
> When evil men assail me ...
> it is they, my foes and my enemies,
> who stumble and fall....
> One thing I ask of *Adonai*,
> only that do I seek:
> to live in the house of *Adonai*
> all the days of my life,
> to gaze upon the beauty of *Adonai*....
> Now is my head high
> over my enemies roundabout;
> I sacrifice in His tent with shouts of joy,
> singing and chanting a hymn to *Adonai*....
> Do not forsake me, do not abandon me,
> O God, my deliverer,
> Though my father and mother abandon me,
> *Adonai* will take me in.
> Do not subject me to the will of my foes,
> For false witnesses and unjust accusers

have appeared against me.
Wait on *Adonai*,
be of good courage
and He shall strengthen your heart.
Wait, I say, on *Adonai*.

(Psalm 27:1–2, 4, 6, 9b–10, 12, 14)

This text is traditionally read each morning of Elul, the Hebrew month that comes immediately before Rosh Hashanah, the Jewish New Year, and then read each day through Simchat Torah, the celebration of concluding and restarting the reading of the Torah. The psalm begins with a mood of gentle confidence: "*Adonai* is my light." When you have no artificial illumination, to have light is no small matter, as when after many cloudy days, we are deeply grateful for the sun. *Adonai* is also described as my help, which sounds pretty ordinary in English. Unfortunately, here our translators fail us. The word in Hebrew, *vayishi*, implies a special sense of release that we feel after we've been in trouble but now are all right. Perhaps we should imagine that the psalmist is in a dark place but knows that the Ultimate Power and Wisdom of the universe will be lighting the way, and so has the poetic confidence to say: "Of whom should I be afraid?"

This same mood is then expressed in a different metaphor, "*Adonai* is the stronghold of my life." The psalmist, like many others in this biblical book, will soon describe life's difficulties as being beset by his foes. He now moves to a martial metaphor and speaks of God as the fortress protecting a life under attack. "When evil men assail me, it is they"—because God is on my side—"who stumble and fall." Confidence intensifies with such protection. The poet now goes all out and says, "One thing I ask of *Adonai* … to live in the house of *Adonai* all the days of my life." God being what God is, if I could just be there together with God all the time, that's all I ask. In those circumstances, of course, "Now is my head high over my enemies" and, therefore, "I'll gladly sacrifice in His tent with shouts of joy, singing and chanting a hymn."

There is something excessive going on. Of course, I'm not so much reading the psalm as I am reading myself, which is what one of the world's greatest religious poems ought to do. My moods sometimes shift this way. One minute I'm feeling terrific and on top of the world and two seconds later I'm down in the dumps. I know that I'll probably feel better soon but I can't be absolutely confident about it. And the same thing is as true of religious certainties as it is of personal assurances. For the moment I am full of religious confidence because of this wonderful spiritual intimacy I'm feeling with God.

Then, suddenly, whatever had been concealed by my excessive emotion comes rushing out: "Do not forsake me [God], do not abandon me … though my father and mother abandon me," don't You do the same thing to me! Phew! One needn't be a psychoanalyst to hear the deep-seated fear in these words. The fear of abandonment is one of childhood's most damaging experiences, psychologists tell us. Now my greatest fear emerges: "Do not abandon me to the will of my foes." This anxiety about enemies arises frequently in the Book of Psalms, apparently because in those days, despite all the strength of the poets' belief and love and trust in God, a lack of security was so common that faith was continually being threatened by it.

The Psalms have taught that more than three thousand years ago, there were people who could speak movingly of a religiosity that shifted between the confidence and fear I recognize in myself. Is it any wonder that this biblical book speaks to me with a special, sacred intimacy?

Because its poems speak in and to many moods, the Book of Psalms continues to be a rewarding companion for aiding spiritual life. Whether the soul seeks uplift or protest, stimulus or quiet, people through the ages and throughout the world find these beautiful, uplifting words conversing in beautiful, measured speech.

28

Reliving the Sinai Experience Each Year

Shavuot, a holiday celebrating the giving of the Torah, is proba-bly the Jewish festival with the least appeal these days. Of course Passover has its much-beloved seder, and even though Sukkot, the fall harvest festival, comes so soon after the High Holy Days, it stands out because of its open-roofed hut and that unique business of waving a palm branch while holding a lemony citron. But poor Shavuot! All it has are blintzes—and that for reasons that no one can sensibly give. So let me try to explain why Shavuot deserves to be cherished—which is in itself another indication of its offbeat character.

Any time religious leaders have to give elaborate discussions of why people should do something, it's a sure sign that people aren't doing it. The most reasonable validation of an observance should arise not from abstract discussions but from participation—"try it; you'll like it"—a test I'll apply to Shavuot in due course. But theology junky that I am, I think it is important to say a few words about the beliefs behind the practice.

The problem of Shavuot for liberal Jews is both verbal and doctrinal. The fundamental rabbinic belief is that at Mt. Sinai, God gave Moses not only the Written Torah (or Written Law, the Bible's Five Books of Moses), but also the Oral Torah (or Oral Law), the rules that authorized future scholars, the Rabbis, to modify, extend, or even innovate what Jews must do.

The difficulty with the biblical story of Sinai is not that it isn't historical. The difficulty with the story is what it says: Never before and never again, God speaks out loud and gives ten "instructions" to the fleeing Israelite ex-slaves. That's what the Book of Exodus tells us, and it continues with an entirely plausible account of the people's reaction. They are terrified, and they petition Moses to ask God to give the rest of the Divine demands directly to him. "You speak to us," they say to Moses, "and we will obey; but let not God speak to us, lest we die" (Exodus 20:16).

The esteemed twentieth-century philosopher and theologian Abraham Joshua Heschel devoted his intellectual career to trying to convince moderns that they ought to accept the fact of God's Revelation as described in the Bible. Yet even he had difficulties with this important concept. He attempted to explain in *God in Search of Man* that when the Bible records a revelation, it is accurate, but when the Bible talks *about* the revelation process, it is midrash, imaginative reconstruction. If this quintessentially God-centered philosopher is reduced to making such a hairsplitting distinction, liberal Jews should feel no shame in owning up to a spiritual disconnect concerning the miraculous Revelation at Sinai.

Modernized Jews think of the entire Bible as a series of creative imaginings, interpreting the God-experiences of our people's great religious figures. To be less pedantic, with all the love and respect I and many others have for Jewish tradition, it is unbelievable that God reveals God's Self in words. Even in moments I have been closest and most intimate with God, I haven't heard *Adonai* speaking in any literal sense of the term. To the contrary, it is deeply disturbing when someone claims that God has literally talked to him or her and has authorized some pretty outlandish things.

Positively put, I believe that our knowledge of God is experiential, a human response to God's presence, rather than objective, a noninterfering human reception of God's instructions. This notion of Revelation as a Divine-human partnership grounds my intuition that traditional Jewish law and custom must sometimes give way to what the faithful liberal community perceives as its God-given duty.

As a result, although I cannot commemorate the giving of the Torah as traditional Judaism understands it, I celebrate the establishment and continual renewal of the relationship between God and Israel. I affirm the Covenant as the foundation of my existence and acknowledge that truth when I respectfully stand under "the Law." Only for me, as for most modernized Jews, the Law is not simply the Written or the Oral Law of our tradition. The Law is the living discipline that flows from being in direct personal relationship with God as a member of the covenanted community. I cannot agree that the pact established at Sinai between God and the people of Israel is immutable, for new social circumstances and intellectual insights may well transform and enhance traditional patterns. I also know that a relationship is meaningful only as it results in action, and Covenant without responsibility, faith without deed, is meaningless.

The Shavuot confirmation ceremony was created by modern Jews and involves teens who celebrate the approaching end of their childhood by speaking to the congregation and affirming their Jewish faith. The fact that this lovely ritual occurs on Shavuot appeals to me because its practice also serves as its justification. Each year the Sinai day rolls around and the faithfulness of Israel to our ancient pledge is once more tested and once again renewed. Our children celebrate being part of all the children of Israel by this public, formal rededication. We have done our duty by helping them to know our precious, sacred history. We now invite our confirmands to personally assume our messianic task.

This is why the assembled congregation is so moved. Of course it may be sentiment mixed with guilt, the conscious realization of our aging fused with the illusions we sometimes associate with our children. Yet these emotions are worthy of bearing God's truth and sensitizing us to God's presence. We may not have been the Jews we ought to have been, the Jews that our parents or grandparents or rabbis had wished us to be. But on this Shavuot day in the sanctuary, seeing our children on God's bimah, the area at the front of a synagogue's sanctuary, and hearing them affirm and avow and depose and declare, we know we have not been altogether faithless. By bringing them to confirmation, we have confirmed our own loyalty; by confirming them, we are confirmed as well.

That is true not only for the parents of confirmands but for every Jew who identifies with the Jewish community and shares in its mutual responsibility for the education of Jewish children. These confirmands are all our children, the next necessary link in our people's purposeful preservation. Celebrating Sinai in this way actualizes our hope that our Covenant effort will continue, working and waiting for God's dominion to be made real among us.

29

"Weighing" the Texts That Instruct Us

As rabbis and laity increasingly turn to classic Jewish texts for help in dealing with the dilemmas of our time, it becomes important to face the reality that all texts were not created equal. Some "carry more weight" in decision making than others. That was true for the ancient Rabbis—the texts' transmitters—and for all who wish to understand what our forebears thought.

Let me give a quick American civics analogy. Citations from the Declaration of Independence have more influence on us than do the more mundane correspondence of Thomas Jefferson or James Madison, but none of these normally defines American duty as decisively as does our Constitution.

In a similar way, thoughtful Jews seeking assistance from their tradition must find both the pertinent classic texts that treat their problem and also get a sense of the extent of authority that the Rabbis likely attached to them. This isn't easy. Four diverse examples may help illustrate what is involved.

The first and best-known practice is to distinguish halachah (rabbinic texts whose imperatives are considered mandatory) from aggadah (rabbinic texts whose teachings are only highly commended). It sometimes takes considerable learning to distinguish one from the other. If in a series of Talmudic accounts we read that

Hillel the Elder, a distinguished teacher of the early days of the rabbinic tradition, gave a recently impoverished heir a horse and a slave to run before it (Babylonian Talmud, K'tubot 67b), would a modern interpretation of that text require our Jewish federations to restore a Bentley to a once-rich family now languishing in bankruptcy? Or should we not rather take this and other accounts of our Rabbis' customary exaggeration as aggadic, in this case simply admonishing us to try to preserve the dignity of the poor?

Often we can tell one kind of discourse from the other by how later teachers have interpreted them. But this is complicated by the fact that, when no good halachic analogies were available, later Sages might have based their legal rulings on an aggadic text, even though aggadic texts are only rarely used in traditional Jewish decision making.

A second sort of "weighing" problem arose in a contemporary rabbinic legal opinion that required a sibling who was found to be a suitable donor to give another sibling a desperately needed kidney for a transplant. Here the mode of discussion is entirely halachic, but the relevant texts, acknowledging that this is an extraordinary act, speak in terms of *hesed*, that untranslatable term whose meanings include kindheartedness, loving-kindness, benevolence, and mercy. The traditional discussions end by making this act of *hesed* required, while today we would probably think it a contradiction to consider benevolence compulsory. Although the text is clear, the logic is not, which will surely influence the weight we moderns give texts like this one.

A third source of perplexity arises when what seems a reasonably clear practice or idea is authorized by a text from a less-than-central book. For example, the Torah leaves no doubt that Jews are commanded to give to charity; abstaining altogether from this deed is a major sin. It is only a modest step from Torah to Talmudic dicta that the local institution that collects and disburses charity, the community *bet din*, also has the power to coerce reluctant Jews to contribute properly. The twelfth-century philosopher Maimonides decides similarly in his pioneering Jewish law code, the *Mishneh Torah*, literally, *The Torah [Law] Restated*. That book being so important to later generations, it is somewhat jarring to find a writer who might validate this community practice merely by quoting from a legally marginal work, the thirteenth-century account of a Germanic mystic group, *The Book of the Pietists*, *Sefer Hasidim*. Mentioning only this peripheral citation will lessen the weight we attach to the notion of the Jewish community's coercive power to collect charity, while citing the *Mishneh Torah* alone would provide a firm foundation for the authority of the *bet din*.

The fourth difficulty arises when one is seeking classic Jewish guidance on a critical matter like warfare, where ancient rabbinic law was clearly more hypothetical than practical, and only more recently in the State of Israel has become a matter of realpolitik. To be sure, the halachic process has itself long distinguished between reasoning carried out as an act of Torah study, a theoretical scholarly exercise, and something that is mandated duty, *halachah lema'aseh*.

But it is one thing to elaborate on the law when you have no authority to convict or punish anyone and quite another thing when you do have that power. So although we certainly can learn a great deal from classic texts when trying to ascertain the Jewish attitudes toward war, we may be better served giving greater weight to contemporary interpretations.

These four examples should make plain that the process of learning from Jewish tradition inevitably involves a measure of subjectivity. Some will with good reason weigh the texts one way; others, with equal validity, will weigh them quite differently. Anyone with a serious question about what the Jewish tradition taught about a given matter would want to be involved in the process: Orthodox Jews, to determine what their God-given duty is; and non-Orthodox Jews, to learn what guidance Jewish tradition could offer them. When the issue is serious and an informed response is sought, we seek the help of someone with much Jewish learning and textual experience. However, any thoughtful person can get a significant taste of this process by reading or studying one of the many English works that discuss modern subjects and provide samples of relevant rabbinic opinion.

Putting Texts in Context

30

A textually rich presentation I heard in synagogue one Friday night at first pleased me, yet later left me somewhat troubled. The speaker wanted to show the many textual roots of Jewish commitment to social action. He presented a selection of favorite biblical passages appropriate to the topic and bolstered these with a goodly number of rabbinic statements. Then, having finished, he quickly concluded and sat down.

Two things about his sermon particularly gave me pleasure. I certainly agreed that believing Jews should have a strong social ethic whose horizon reaches far beyond our Jewish community, embracing everyone in some practical way. (Need I add that Judaism, as I understand it, also bids us to take action and not just be satisfied with good intentions?) I was also glad he sought to validate his argument by emphasizing its roots in our tradition.

When I was a young rabbi, more than fifty years ago, my colleagues and I regularly made the case for ethical duty by appealing to every decent person's sense of expected responsibility. In those days, we were eager to think of ourselves as part of humankind, rather than taking Jewish belief or Jewish tradition very seriously. Since then, the tight connection between reason and ethics has largely evaporated, chiefly because we have witnessed the evil that highly intelligent people are capable of doing. Besides, it's fairly clear that people are more significantly shaped by groups they feel part of—in our case, the Jewish people—than by pure reason. So our preacher appealed to us "where we live" by citing a plethora of Jewish guidance from over the centuries.

Then I began to have second thoughts. Listening to his cascade of texts, those of us in the congregation might well conclude that all of Jewish teaching advocated this activist concern for humanity. However, shouldn't leaders, especially when speaking about ethics, make an effort to be as historically accurate as possible? Premodern Jews, outsiders in the communities in which they lived and often victims of persecution there, were mostly quite parochial in their concerns. They were far more invested in getting along with their governments than in changing or redirecting their basic political philosophy. Anyone who believes in the ethics of self-defense will understand this stance. Moreover, is it not true that today's traditionally observant Jews, the ones who seek to live by the sacred literature, may hold quite different social concerns than liberal Jews do? Liberal Jews have been chided by more traditional Jews for insisting that Jewish tradition inspires us to support governmental initiatives that may benefit society as a whole but often in the short run seem to go against our particular Jewish interests (the classic case—financing public but not parochial education).

The liberal Jewish commitment to social justice for all doesn't stem from a simple political bias; rather, it comes from a strong shift in our social horizons. Having suffered the diminution of personhood that comes from being cast as social pariahs, premodern Jews thought mainly in terms of Jewish survival. Once governments in the nineteenth century began giving Jews rights as equal citizens, some courageous, even prophetic souls dared to enlarge the old sense of Jewish duty. As the social and political barriers began to fall away, slowly to be sure, Jews became full members of their societies. Farsighted thinkers transformed old, largely self-centered ethics to more expansively include all those created in God's image. This made the messianic dream of a united humanity a possible contemporary ideal.

Once this shift in status began, the Jewish people started to read their sacred texts with new sensitivity. What was astonishing then, and has remained a matter of quiet Jewish pride to this day, is how often we moderns have discovered a broader ethics in texts that were initially shaped by a narrower need for self-protection. We remember, although we often take for granted, that our God does not care only for our people. The Eternal is the only One, and thus a part of everyone created in God's image. Given the opportunity, this vision has made itself felt again and again in our teaching and our laws.

So I wish that along with the textual riches our Friday-night speaker brought us, he had also told something of this inspiring intellectual story. By leaving it out—or assuming everyone knew it—he left himself open to the charge that he himself had committed an ethical lapse. He gave the incorrect sense that Jewish writing was overflowing with a universal ethical commitment. In Jewish terms, that sin is called *genevat da'at*, giving a false impression. He could have avoided *genevat da'at* by explaining even briefly that the texts he offered were beloved by contemporary liberal Jewry, which glories in goals of worldwide democracy, not community-based ethics of a bygone age.

I hasten to add that I fully agree with the speaker's way of reading our tradition, showing the relevance of ancient texts in today's world. I am only eager to avoid the impression that his is the only way to present these marvelous old sacred texts—as if they did not have an equal and overriding concern to conserve ancient tradition. But since I believe that Jewish truth has grown in modernity, as I believe it did in the past—liberal Jew that I am—I am happy to see today's teachers discerning in our old texts the long-buried truths that speak to contemporary issues. However, since liberal

Jews are strong partisans of Jewish ethics, I believe they have a special responsibility to indicate that the liberal way of reading the Jewish past is not the only way that caring and learned Jews do so today.

31

Religious Authority in Judaism

The election of Benedict XVI as pope in 2005 assured the stability and continuity of the Roman Catholic Church, with its billion-plus members. In total contrast, consider the Jews. Just how did we Jews manage to maintain our own particular religious identity, when in addition to having no centralized institutional structure, we kept arguing about what we should do and believe? People often talk about the Jewish will to survive, and we have certainly seen great evidence of that. While I am not equipped to say much about the social mechanisms that enabled us to continue, we can gain some insight into this remarkable achievement by considering the various beliefs about religious authority that have emerged among Jews during our history. In my mind's eye, I see this as a development with five major stages. Herewith is my imaginative account of what transpired.

Biblical Revelation, what God told our people, is the foundation of all religious power and influence in Judaism. Directly stated, if God said it, people should do it. But for all God's status and supremacy, God is good enough to give people unique freedom to do or not to do God's will. Of course, if we disobey or sin, God will likely punish us, as happened to the generation of the Flood, the ungrateful Exodus complainers (particularly Korach and his family), and the Jews who settled the Promised Land only to turn to idolatry again and again.

The climax of this period of God's direct involvement in Jewish destiny is the Babylonian conquest of the Kingdom of Judah in 597 and 586 BCE, with the consequent destruction of the Temple and subsequent exile of the people. But God is also greatly forgiving, thus the regular Temple rites for the forgiveness of sin and the annual Day of Atonement, as well as numerous statements about God's abounding mercy. "*Adonai* is compassionate and gracious, slow to anger, abounding in steadfast love" (Psalms 103:8). In 534 the exiles were allowed to return to their land, and they finally rebuilt the Temple in 520 BCE. Roughly, this is the Bible's revealed view of God's effective authority.

How God's power became humanly institutionalized in biblical times is not clear. As in much of the Ancient Near East, each Jewish town governed itself by appointing its own judiciary—elders who settled disputes at the city gate. As related in Deuteronomy17:8–10, "If a matter is too difficult for you, go and appear before the levitical priests or the magistrate in charge at the time.... You shall carry out the verdict that they announce to you from that place that *Adonai* has chosen, observing scrupulously all their instructions to you." That's about all the data concerning localized authority that we have. We know even less about how monarchs exercised their power locally.

In the **Rabbinic Period** (about 100 BCE–1000 CE), this mix of commandment and freedom is understood in terms of the Oral Law, the verbal instructions that God is understood to have given Moses atop Mount Sinai. The content and method of expansion of the Oral Law were codified, expanded, and eventually written down as the effective means of understanding and applying the Written Torah. The Talmud, its chief document, promoted a unique dialectic of argument and authoritative decision making, a pluralism that strove to generate binding rules, or halachah, that would guide Jewish actions. While rabbinic Sages, the religious masters of this period, occasionally met and voted for this or that to become law, what mostly became required apparently arose out of general usage and consensus.

The Rabbis of the Talmud remembered that before the destruction of the Second Temple in 70 CE, there were local courts of three judges, district courts of twenty-three judges, and the supreme authority, the Sanhedrin, composed of seventy judges. Unfortunately, we have no contemporaneous data on these. While the Rabbis had the power to innovate as well as to transmit traditional law, such rulings applied almost entirely to people's actions rather than to their beliefs. However, the Sages did excoriate their arch-heretic, Elishah ben Abuyah, the onetime great rabbinic teacher of Talmudic times, who is immortalized in Milton Steinberg's classic novel, *As a Driven Leaf*. The Rabbis also kept the Book of Ben Sirach, among other then-popular spiritual writings, from being canonized as part of the Bible. Rabbinic authority, spotty in the early days, increased through the centuries, later becoming what chiefly unified the Jews as they dispersed throughout the known world.

The **Pre-Modern Period** (1000–1800 CE), was the high point of effective rabbinic authority. Already in the tenth century, Saadiah Gaon (*gaon* was the title given him as the rabbinic head of the post-Talmudic academy of Sura), wielded such strong influence that most of world Jewry followed his opinion, for example, that the Karaites (Jewish biblicists who rejected the Oral Torah) should be treated as heretics. Yet typically, some Ashkenazic (of central and eastern European) and almost all Sephardic (of the Mediterranean and North Africa) rabbis permitted Jews to "intermarry" with them.

No small factor in this growth of rabbinic authority came from the increase in local community influence and power. With anti-Jewish persecution ever increasing, the need for Jewish solidarity was critical. Such rights as people had in those days were given to the community, not to individuals; refusing to follow communal norms was therefore perilous. During this time the seminal rabbinic law codes appeared: Maimonides' *Mishneh Torah* (*The Torah Restated*); Jacob ben Asher's *Arba'ah Turim* (*Four Columns*); Joseph Karo's Sephardic *Shulchan Aruch* (*The Set Table*) and its Ashkenazic commentary, Moses Isserles's *Mappah* (*Tablecloth*). The advent of printing made these unifying codes, their later commentaries, and the local expert responses to practical questions about the law, *t'shuvot*, more widely available. Kabbalist teachings enhanced the virtues of observance by postulating that what was done in this world affected the dynamic unity or disunity of God's ten nodes of power and functioning, the *s'firot*. Later, Hasidism intensified this scrupulosity, because each rebbe's reputed special access to God bestowed on his community's customs the authority of commandments.

As Jews increasingly entered general society in the **Modern Period** (ca. 1800–ca. 1970), Western values were often substituted for Jewish faith, and the prior structure of rabbinic-communal authority largely collapsed. Human initiative replaced God's unbridled authority; ethics and conscience supplanted Revelation. When rights were granted by the state to its individual citizens, Jewishness became one option among many, with humankind the compelling social matrix. Before the Nazis, many Jews believed that anti-Semitism slowly was losing its virulence. Despite the Holocaust, Americans after World War II demonstrated a passion for universal democracy and often put their trust in a cultured secularity. Thus God could be declared dead; Jewish religious authority, both in its traditional and modern forms, seemed doomed.

However, many Jews finally realized that if educated, cultured Germans could rationally conceive and carry out the Holocaust, modern optimism about human nature seemed truly naive, and religious tradition thus became newly appealing. With the goodness of human nature debunked and philosophical ethics unable to mandate duty, the need for a substantial ground of value turned us from the death of God to an affirmation of God, and thus to the postmodern spirituality around us. Our era, the **Postmodern Period,** has therefore witnessed a resurgence of all kinds of religious orthodoxies. Despite society's rightward shift, the bulk of the Jewish community remains highly modernized and its religiosity, largely due to its strong individualism, is quite diverse.

Five versions of postmodernism's modes of functioning religious authority may daringly be identified. First, a universalistic, individualistic spirituality whose ethical commitments arise from God's own goodness. Second, individuals grounded in self and community who therefore share in the Jewish people's commanding relationship with God. Third, the feminist regard for the particular as the foundation of the universal, with central attention given to issues of gender. Fourth, an eclectic trust in the tradition when interpreted as modernized ethics. Fifth, a renewed mystical sensitivity to charismatic teachers and the commanding depth of Jewish inwardness.

It is too early to say how demanding a pattern of Jewish observance will arise in any of these positions except right-wing Orthodoxy, which I would place, with an inversion of the religious terms, in the second option. Nonetheless, the existence and fervor of these styles is surely an indication of a modest resurgence of Jewish religious authority today. It is true that liberal Jews continue to spurn a central religious authority, and most of us have no group or figure whose rulings we consider binding. Yet many more of us today than anyone would have anticipated some twenty-five years ago have made Jewish faith and practice a significant aspect of our lives.

32

Integrating Jewish Law and Jewish Ethics

I once wrote that I believed some scholars overstated the place of ethics in halachah as applied to non-Orthodox duty—mitzvah—and what liberal Jews really ought to do. In response, one such scholar asked me, "Does not classic halachah contain an ethical concern?"

The answer, of course, depends on what is meant by "an ethical concern." Since I am not a scholar of Jewish law, I rely on the views of one of the great Talmudists and eminent writers on Jewish law of our time, Rabbi David Weiss Halivni. He said that he does not know of a significant *posek* (someone whose halachic rulings are considered to be authoritative) who mentions ethics or conscience when making a halachic ruling. That means we cannot normally find references to ethics in Jewish case law, *t'shuvot*, our chief evidence for understanding the development of the halachah.

What does matter to these authorities is what legal precedent requires or allows, not what conscience obligates. Behind this procedure is a major religious conviction: Jewish law and its methods—including certain areas that permit differences of opinion—are mandated by God. Only the flexibility that God has built into the process may be utilized by a believing Jew.

That is why, in the face of great ethical pressure to the contrary, some of the most respected halachists of our day will not revise certain humanly troubling Jewish laws. For example, suppose a woman comes to the daily morning service at her traditional synagogue to say the mourner's Kaddish, an Aramaic prayer praising God that a mourner is commanded to recite for a parent. If there are only nine men present, Jewish law says that despite the high ethical and ritual virtue of her intention, she may not be counted as the tenth person needed to make up the minyan, the quorum of ten men required for a full Jewish service. If no man appears to complete the legal quorum, the mourner's Kaddish will not be said at this service. So goes the traditional understanding.

To non-Orthodox Jews, the power of the ethical to override nonethical considerations—from this perspective, much of Jewish law—makes these considerations particularly precious. We feel God's presence in what our conscience demands that we do in order to increase the human good. We have been confirmed in this conviction because our ethical Jewish life styles enable us to live as equals in the general society. Thus a passion for ethics links us closely to God and to all humankind.

With ethics so central to liberal religiosity, we are able to find significant traces of it in classic Jewish teaching. The prophets indicted Israel for its moral, not its ritual infractions; Jonah complained when God forgave the hated Assyrians in Nineveh, who turned away from their evil deeds. The Rabbis provided a prayer for the High Holy Days whose major plea for forgiveness, the Avinu Malkeinu, mostly details sins against other persons, not infractions of ritual law. We avidly collect instances of halachic change where we can detect an ethical impulse struggling to be set free.

Moreover, ethics has a commanding power. This permits the virtue of human fulfillment to override for liberal Jews such traditional commands as where and what we eat, the prohibition against driving to synagogue on Shabbat for communal prayer and study, and the inability to turn on electric switches to read or listen to ennobling music. It was this commitment to ethics that required us, once we realized our unethical treatment of women, to radically change our attitude toward their proper place in our communities. Most of us now take for granted that female rabbis and cantors lead us in prayer and female scholars and executives head large Jewish organizations. For the same reason, we are deeply disturbed that women still do not receive the same compensation as men do in similar jobs. We believe that ethics has so much power in our non-Orthodox Jewish lives that, in these and many more instances, our sacred duties to God are better completed by performing these mitzvot rather than less socially compelling, albeit halachic ones.

Unless I misunderstood the scholar who questioned me, it seems he would impose strong limits on how far "ethical concern" should go in changing certain aspects of classic Jewish law. I am reasonably confident that he was deeply disturbed by what ethics has led a good number of American rabbis to do. Precisely because they see their Jewish ethics validating the serious choices of thoughtful human beings, an ever-growing number of non-Orthodox rabbis now perform intermarriages, and our American non-Orthodox seminaries now accept homosexual students. For similar reasons, Reform and Reconstructionist Jews consider a child born to a Jewish father and non-Jewish mother Jewish when the child has been Jewishly educated and raised in a home that celebrates Jewish rituals and life cycles. In addition, a healthy proportion of these rabbis happily sanctifies the lifelong commitment of two Jews of the same sex by officiating at their weddings. Despite a strong commitment to ethics as a concern of the halachah, my questioner opposed all of these actions and probably would say they are halachically invalid.

I and other dissenting colleagues do these things precisely because performing these rituals are matters of conscience to us. We do not allow traditional strictures of the law to override our sense of right and wrong. If we believed that God was the sole authority behind the halachah, though we might feel conflicted, we would surely insist on God's word remaining supreme. But we *don't* believe God to be the effective power behind stated Jewish law; we insist there is a strong human element in the shaping of the halachah. Thus we have the theoretical burden of explaining how good liberal Jews should integrate our commanding ethics with a Jewish legal tradition that also still substantially defines us.

When I published a book-length series of papers by my students that deal with this puzzle, two divergent reactions were expressed. Our invited, non-Reform reader pointed out how difficult it was for the students to treat the halachic tradition as an equal partner once they took ethics seriously. However, a distinguished Reform colleague, long active in this field, was deeply disturbed because so much attention was given to those positions of contemporary ethicists! I had, of course, insisted that my students give socially conservative and ethical liberal deliberations the same attention they gave to halachah. And I still feel that way.

33

Jewish Decision Making

In the near half century that I have been teaching seminary students, few questions have troubled me more than those dealing with rabbinic decision making. I have offered courses on different approaches to the topic, sometimes with colleagues whose expertise seemed particularly relevant, but mostly on my own. These courses required students to choose a question that might arise in their own lives and write a formal rabbinic answer (a *t'shuvah*, "responsa"). Two that I have received always seem to exemplify what learned, thoughtful rabbinic teaching might beneficially do for a serious inquirer as well as also show the limits inherent in this process.

The two students involved in the first paper—working in partnership enabled them to expand their research and, by discussing it, to refine their reasoning—chose to focus on whether a synagogue should accept ethically tainted gifts. Not surprisingly, there was considerable Jewish literature on this topic throughout the centuries, with the discussion tracing back to the Torah's injunction in Deuteronomy 23:19 not to bring a "whore's hire" to the house of God: "You shall not bring the fee of a whore or the pay of a dog [male prostitute] into the house of *Adonai* your God ... for both are abhorrent to *Adonai* your God."

Determining just what the equivalent was in different times and places was a major concern of Jewish legal authorities. Although this was clearly the religious ideal, it does not take much imagination to see how the answer might clash with the reality of synagogue needs. This issue of the practical—of the great and continuous Jewish need for funds—was given additional weight by a study that the students themselves conducted of the current guidelines put in place by the major Jewish philanthropic agencies. In some cases, anecdotal communication from agency executives added a personal touch to the students' findings. The two students further expanded their thinking by consulting what little had been written on the topic by contemporary ethicists.

I emphasize these details of the student study because it is critical to remember that serious questions deserve seriously thoughtful answers. Moreover, the response must always reflect the gravity that accompanies our serving God as best we can. In this particular case—the synagogue badly needed a new roof and a substantial donation, conditioned on a public, High Holy Days acknowledgment from someone with mob connections—the students ruled that the gift be respectfully rejected.

The second case dealt with genetic engineering. Specifically, it raised the question of the proper Jewish religious attitude toward scientists' identifying the single gene causing the always-fatal Tay-Sachs disease and replacing it with a healthy gene.

After completing a study of relevant Jewish law—a considerable literature exists and continues to be written on bioethical topics—the students summarized the reasons for proceeding with or desisting from a highly controversial medical procedure. According to their reading, Jewish law generally was negative but did contain some basis for a positive response. The students' ethical discussion yielded six reasons to proceed: it heals; it improves the gene pool; it treats both this child and the progeny; it seems the "natural" thing to do; it improves on evolution; and it honors the individual's right to choose. The students also found five reasons against gene replacement: it sets us on a slippery slope toward even greater gene modification; it violates respect for life; it "plays God"; it denies the role of chance in evolution; it changes the gene pool, perhaps irreversibly.

In this case, faced with the same material, the two students differed on what should be done. One student felt that God's presence in the biological flow of life was too great for us to interfere in this genetic stage. The other reasoned that if there could be safeguards against causing later, greater harm, the incentive of curing this cruel disease, Tay-Sachs, required us to "choose life, if you and your offspring would live" (Deuteronomy 30:19).

It often happens in dealing with specific problems that scholars will reach different conclusions. Judaism, unlike some other religions, does not have a mechanism for resolving diversity among its experts. While it is possible that the majority of authoritative rabbis will take a certain stand or even come to consensus, according to rabbinic custom it is not possible to exclude the Jewish validity of differing with these rabbis. To me it seems clear that this Jewish openness to diverse interpretation of the law testifies to subjectivity in the halachic, Jewish legal process.

Several decades ago, the man who became the (Orthodox) Chief Rabbi of the British Empire commented on my point of view by denying that there was ever a personal factor in Jewish decision making. He attributed the diversity to what God had inspired particular scholars to "see" at a given time. Non-Orthodox rabbis have made a greater place for the personal factor. They have tried to limit what Isaac Mayer Wise, the founder of institutional American Reform Judaism, once notably called the "presumptuous innovations and the precipitations of rash and inconsiderate men." The Conservative Rabbinical Assembly has a Commission on Jewish Law and Standards whose unanimous decisions are binding on all Conservative rabbis, and whose split decisions authorize varied opinions, with local rabbis able to specify which is binding in their particular communities. Reform rabbis have a somewhat similar Responsa Committee but its decisions, though influential, are only advisory.

In my own view, the regard for the single self has been too important a factor in furthering human fulfillment not to give it, in its sense of "divine image," a major place when faced with the ultimate hopes and challenges of our lives. However, Judaism has long understood individuality as grounded in God and the Jewish people's ancient bond with the Eternal. Thus those who seek Jewish teaching on a critical problem occurring in their lives or in their communities should not only look for a learned, thoughtful rabbi's guidance but for a rabbi whose personal piety and dedication illumine the response.

34

Innovation in Judaism: Yesterday and Today

Some people have been unhappy with my saying that the kind of innovations in practice that modern Jews initiated—like praying in the vernacular or permitting driving to shul for Shabbat services—were major breaks with prior Jewish patterns of change, that is, those we find in the Talmud and that continue today in Orthodoxy, with special emphasis on precedent. I know most of my non-Orthodox colleagues like to argue that change, even great change, was characteristic of this style of interpreting Jewish law. They can give some impressive examples of this, such as allowing the specifically oral traditions of God's law to be written down; or, in later years, ruling that a divorce would be valid only if the woman about to be divorced was willing to accept the divorce document. So why do I hold a view that sounds more like that held by Orthodox critics of liberal Jews than one agreeing with the mainstream of my own community?

The short answer is that I think it is historically more accurate. And if I may add a religious note, I think that we modernizing Jews are right to be as radical as we are. To put it grandly: There was a biblical Judaism before rabbinic halachah, and for two centuries now we have been creating a post- (but not anti-) halachic Judaism.

I don't deny, particularly in the early centuries of the rabbinic legal system, that there were some remarkable instances of innovation.

Much of this rested on the rabbinic belief, unknown to the Bible, that God revealed not only a Written Torah but also an Oral Torah at Sinai. This authorized the Rabbis to interpret the Torah as they saw fit, often deriving new teachings. Through the ages, our continuing rabbinic tradition allowed Jews to remain faithful to what God had told our people at Sinai while encouraging them to read our sacred text in ever-new depth and spirit. This, too, is the reason that modern Orthodoxy is not rigidly fundamentalist but retains a certain flexibility in interpreting what God demands of us.

Equally, I believe classic Jewish legal creativity arose from the need of any legal system to keep adapting as the realities of life change, the classic example being the innovative Jewish legal document (called a *prosbul*) created by Hillel, the great teacher of the early Talmudic tradition. This document assigned loans between Jews to the court, thereby allowing observant Jews to carry a debt past the sabbatical year, even though the Torah called for all such loans to be forgiven then. Without such creative lawmaking, an increasingly cash economy would threaten to slow down drastically as the seventh year of the sabbatical cycle approached, when all debts were cancelled. Ritually, too, the substituting of words of prayer for animal or other sacrifices and the creating of daily synagogue worship services were equally unprecedented.

Moreover, scholars have long noted the remarkable flexibility of Jewish law. Over the centuries, Jewish authorities have not found it necessary to create new institutional structures that would have slowed further development. The consensus of the learned community was as close as one could come to seeking "the" authoritative stand of Jewish law on a disputed topic. Two historical and one contemporary example come to mind. A little more than a thousand years ago, Rabbenu Gershom, a major legal authority living in Franco-German lands, outlawed polygamy in his community, and the rest of Ashkenazic (central and eastern European) Jewry came to accept his ruling. Several centuries later, the mystic recitation of

Psalms to welcome Shabbat, called *Kabbalat Shabbat,* became the standard prelude to Friday-night Sabbath services. And in our own day, anyone who has tried to keep abreast of the flood of halachic writing on bioethics, such as when an abortion or an experimental operation or an end-of-life procedure may be performed, must be impressed with the passionate erudition and human sensitivity applied to issues unanticipated by the great halachists of earlier generations. As I understand the history of Jewish law, this much, at least, can be said in defense of its ongoing flexibility.

Here, however, is what troubles me about much non-Orthodox writing regarding the openness of Jewish law: In their eagerness to justify their innovations, many modern writers overstate the case for the law's openness. I suggest that we will have a truer picture of halachah if we view it like Isaac Newton's rule: for every action, there must be an equal and opposite reaction. I rarely can find contemporary authors who advance the idea of rabbinic legal creativity who also describe the contrasting patterns of control and restriction. The simple truth would seem to be that the history of Jewish law before modern times is marked more by continuity than by change, and by an increasing concern for precedent rather than a celebration of creativity.

Let me now balance my previous examples of innovation by invoking the classic instance of Jewish law's inability to change: the *agunah,* literally "the chained woman." She cannot be divorced and is unable to remarry except by the free will of her husband; he, for spite or more venal reasons, refuses to divorce her. For generations now, though halachists and challengers alike agree that every human consideration demands this divorce, and despite many ingenious halachic proposals over the past couple of centuries, many women today remain *agunot.* Here Jewish law exposes its inflexible side. Many other, less heartbreaking examples could be given.

Observers of law have commonly noted that legal systems characteristically tend to conserve rather than to innovate. This seems true of Jewish law as well. But in the case of Jewish law, there is an additional factor to be considered: halachah is what God demands of us. Already in the twelfth century, Maimonides, the greatest Jewish thinker of the Middle Ages, made this quite plain in his pathbreaking code of Jewish law, the *Mishneh Torah* (*The Torah Restated*). In the section on the laws of repentance (3.8), he indicates that to deny that the Torah as a whole, or one of its verses, or even a single letter was composed by Moses and was not God's revelation would render a person a heretic, worthy of *cherem*, the Jewish equivalent of excommunication. To be sure, Maimonides is speaking here more of belief than of practice; however, by putting divine authority behind every letter of the law, his interest in meticulous observance is unmistakable.

Were right-wing Orthodoxy ever to rise to political as well as religious power in the State of Israel, it is not clear how tolerant they would be of what, by their traditional Jewish legal standards, would be considered non-Orthodox sinfulness. As it is, their refusal to sanction a non-Orthodox Israeli rabbi to officiate at marriages or conversion ceremonies sticks in the craw of most liberal Jews. The North American equivalent of the situation in Israel is the current battle being waged in some Jewish community centers, operated with community or Jewish federation funds, to open their doors on Saturday afternoons.

All this leads to a final factor in understanding contemporary Jewish creativity—in other words, what Reform Jews like myself seem willing to do. Consider the kinds of changes in Jewish practice that modern times have made widespread: men and women sitting together at services; broader acceptance of cremation as well as burial; *shivah*, the traditional seven-day mourning period, reduced to three days; a virtual abandonment of the second day of most festival observances; keeping kosher at home but allowing some latitude when eating out; women counted in a minyan, the quorum of ten required for a full Jewish service, and serving as rabbis; a welcoming attitude to intermarried families in our congregations; and an openness to homosexuals in our seminaries and communities. Today, these and other innovations are common in many non-Orthodox communities.

Why? Because most modern liberal Jews believe that the Torah is substantially a human creation, not mainly God's revelation. That view of the Torah and all that derives from it is a radical break from traditional Judaism. No matter how much liberal Jews try to co-opt classic Jewish creativity to justify their modern view of what God wants of them, I think a creative view of halachah says more about what we believe than what rabbinic Judaism believed or practiced.

V
Thinking about Holiness

Why Do We Need Theology?

35

I have often been asked, "Why do we need theology?" I can think of several good responses to this question, and will get to them; however, in the many years that I have been campaigning for theology, I have often discovered much worrisome baggage attached to the phrase "we need." So I am going to address this matter first.

In 1962 I wrote an article about "our need" for theology. This article broke the unofficial boycott long conducted by non-Orthodox Jewish leaders. Most were quite hesitant about speaking publicly about God, lest they reveal their own widely held feelings of agnosticism. In response to my article, the eminent philosopher Sidney Morgenbesser reminded me that Jews don't have compulsory beliefs, and that I shouldn't try foisting "dogma" on the Jewish community. What I said to him then and still believe today is that in Judaism, theology is a variety of aggadah, the optional portion of Oral Torah, not of halachah, the traditionally mandatory part. Having said that, I want to paraphrase Hai, the last great *Gaon*, or head of the Babylonian Academy of Pumbeditha, who lived a thousand years ago in what is today modern Iraq: "If something in the aggadah makes sense to you, believe it; and if it doesn't, you don't have to."

Let me also add what I consider to be the classic instance of Judaism's uncommonly open attitude toward "needed" beliefs.

147

Almost everyone agrees that Maimonides (1135–1204) was the greatest Jewish philosopher who ever lived. He held that while our most cherished thoughts importantly linked us to God, we still need to think clearly about God and about God's relationship to the Jews, no matter how many *mitzvot* we observe. He set down thirteen concise, indispensable ideas every Jew "needs" to believe. But within a century or so, even these statements were thought to be too long, so two condensed versions became popular. One was intended for people who had finished saying *Shacharit*, the morning service, and wanted to begin the day with some quick study. The other, even shorter version is a song still sung at the end of a service, the Yigdal, a title taken from its opening word. In translation, the poem begins: "How great [*Yigdal*] and praiseworthy is the living God."

A concluding thought about our needing theology: I'm not claiming, or even implying, that the best way to understand Judaism is to delve into its ideas about God, Torah, and Israel. I agree with all those Jews who believe that to know Judaism best, one should live it. Joining in a good Shabbat dinner, or helping to create a little more justice where you work, or making a shivah call (visiting someone in mourning), or participating in other Jewish practices are better introductions to the life of Torah. In sum, unless you have the same kink in your DNA that has driven me and a few others to spend our lives thinking about Jewish religious ideas, you don't have to be a theologian to be a good Jew—*but*, if I may put it baldly, it certainly *isn't* a Jewish virtue to be a brainless Jew.

Now to the subject at hand. For me there are three very good reasons why some Jews, at least, should be thinking very seriously about what they believe. The first is to help keep us from making fools of ourselves. Just because something is called a religion and some people feel very powerfully about its teachings, this doesn't mean it might not lead people to do things that, on reflection, would seem quite odd or even bad. With too much regularity, we have heard or read of such deviant religiosity; the mass suicide of the Jonestown community in 1978 and the massacre in Waco, Texas, in 1993 are only two of the more striking examples.

Like all other people, Jews have discovered in their own communities that no amount of Torah study or Jewish practice can ensure that a person will not do evil. True, our Jewish tradition and our ancient penchant for arguing over everything can protect us from some of that. Yet our religious community, like every other, needs some people who will think very intensely about what constitutes responsible religious belief and practice today. That is a major reason for needing theology. It is not a foolproof safeguard; however, compared to thoughtless religiosity, it has very much indeed to commend it.

Second, our recognition of change as a major factor in our search for truth demands that we cultivate a sense of Ultimate Reality. Should our Judaism be satisfied with anything simpler? Consider the changes in thinking about God that I have seen in my lifetime. In the 1950s we wanted to be as rational as possible about God, and we talked about having a cogent idea or concept of God. That had the advantage of grounding a central commitment to ethics. As our consciousness of the Holocaust grew in the late 1960s and continued into the 1970s, the death-of-God theology demanded that we give up our good God and be fulfilled through ethical living.

Then we arrived at a time when our cold, scientific rationality no longer compelled ethics. Instead, though we never really understood why, we found ourselves searching for compassionate interactions with others, which validated us and confirmed our deep humanity. That gave our religious thinkers a new model for speaking about our "relationship" with God. By the 1990s that disillusion with rationality and turn to the experiential had blossomed into a new openness to Jewish mysticism—a profound personal experience of God—and more recently into what often seems a faddish fascination with Kabbalah. Surely in the midst of such dynamic examinations of the soul, it will be helpful to figure out what teachings make good Jewish sense to us.

The third and perhaps the best reason for thinking long and hard about God and God's relationship with people in general and our people in particular is that it refines our spirituality. Theology—the "ology" or logic about *theos*, the Greek word for God—like poetry or storytelling or ritual-making or studying a sacred text, can be a way of getting closer to God. Whatever else God means to us, God means truth, or, if you prefer, Truth, or even The Truth. This doesn't mean that anyone has any hope of knowing it all. But since what we do know is the most important truth of our lives, we want to keep trying to understand it better and hope that we are getting closer to it.

Years ago, when I told a rabbinic group that the best we could expect in our thinking about God were theologies that were, as I put it, "less inadequate" than their predecessors, I was chided for not saying something more inspiring. I responded: When one is speaking about the Ground of All Existence, that is, as I understand it, the truth.

36

Theology as an Afterthought

Rabbi Zalman Schachter-Shalomi, leader of the Jewish Renewal movement, has stated, "Theology is the afterthought of spiritual experience, not the other way around." Even though I'm not a mystic as he is, I often find that Zalman gets to the heart of being religious in ways the rest of us tend to clog with abstraction or poor imagery. I do understand him—in my own way.

I agree that from biblical days to our own, most people didn't first work out an entire belief system and then find a religion that matched it. Rather, first something stirred the human soul, and only later did a person seek appropriate ways to stay in touch with this uplifting feeling. Spiritual outreach is mostly a matter of attitude and action, not intellectual inquiry. We've all discovered this truism when we're out socializing with someone who, instead of just savoring the meal or appreciating the movie or reaching out to others, is busy analyzing The Experience. An overactive mind can easily keep us from enjoying life's simple pleasures.

Though we Jews have characteristically been proud of our intellectuality, it is piety that our tradition has emphasized. Search the Bible as we will, we won't find anyone who, sensitive to God's presence, ever stepped back to fit that experience into an abstract theory of the universe. Neither the decision of Abraham, the first Jew,

151

who, listening to God, left his idolatrous Mesopotamian city of Ur, nor Moses' barefoot awareness at the burning bush, nor the Moabitess Ruth's determination to accompany her mother-in-law, Naomi, back to Judah, were first worked out as distinct philosophies. Religiosity evolved from peoples' responses to the spiritual, whether as wispy as detected by a baby's gurgle or as grand as a life-altering encounter. Today as in biblical days, people whose spirit has been stirred by the Holy may write poetry, sing, meditate, or reach out to those who need help. In short, no one needs to be a theologian to be a believing Jew.

But that certainly shouldn't be taken to mean that Judaism is mindless. From biblical times to the present, prophets, lawgivers, and other Jewish religious leaders have emphasized the religious priority of sacred living over thinking about the holy. Our greatest teachers, thoughtful biblical and rabbinic souls, applied their minds to creating laws for their societies and institutions, as well as to setting forth general Jewish values to guide those aspects of life that are too fluid for anything but self-determination. Their creativity led to centuries of applied intellectuality.

Inevitably, some of these dedicated types took their role as God's agents so seriously that they obsessively multiplied Jewish duties or the ways in which others might later refine them. Our modern equivalent of such hairsplitting piety causes us to multiply questions to evade participating in ritual or group prayer. We prefer analyzing to doing—often, even to trying—which explains much about why many have such trouble with lasting love.

Why, then, have I spent my life working on Jewish theology? Certainly not because I think such abstract speculation is the best way for Jews to make Judaism the core of their existence. I believe there are good reasons for studying the established explanations of Judaism and creating ones that speak more clearly to the caring soul.

For me, the primary role of intellect in religion is therapeutic. Who hasn't had the unhappy realization of having been taken in by an emotion that appealed to a weakness instead of a strength? There are those who prey on this very gullibility. As the nightly news reminds us, ours is a time of multiple scams, and religious ones abound—and we need our minds to protect us. Thinking about what we are doing, and the reasons that motivate us, is a major though not infallible way of avoiding spiritual regret.

More positively, there is great wisdom in our millennial tradition and remarkable insight in the different ways our contemporary Jewish thinkers have rethought and restated Jewish truths to make them sacred in our contemporary world. I continually run into people whose misunderstandings of Jewish beliefs falsely deprive them of Judaism's continuing holiness. And I have been inspired by numerous others who, having opened their minds to a thinker's reinterpretation of our tradition, have become ennobled by Jewish responsibility.

Besides, we humans are thinking animals. Now and then, we all must give some thought to what we most deeply believe in and live by. I'll be bold—none of us can escape doing a certain amount of theologizing. When Reb Zalman says that theology is an afterthought, he is reasonably serious. But his statement itself is not so much a report *of* his religious experience as it is a thoughtful observation *about* it. To teach us, he must occasionally speak mind-to-mind as well as heart-to-heart. His dismissal of theology's significance for Judaism is self-refuting, for it itself is an exercise in spiritual sensibility and theological imagination.

37

Why Historical
Theology Won't Do

I do not validate my writings on Jewish faith by showing the histor-ical evolution of my ideas, and similarly, I don't include copious citations of relevant Jewish texts. By couching my theology in largely modern terms, am I violating my own demand that those who speak today about Jewish belief do so as members of the people of Israel, with explicit reference to our historic Covenant with God?

In much of the nineteenth and early twentieth centuries, schol-ars had great confidence that studying the history of Judaism would clarify what was considered "truth" in the Judaism of the day. Prior to that period, truth was generally characterized as eternal, unchanging over time. Thus the premodern teachers of history reg-ularly read their current beliefs and customs back into earlier ages. We see that most dramatically in the many medieval pictures of ancient religious worthies clothed in the contemporary dress of the artist's era.

Even before the theory of evolution clinched the case in the mid-nineteenth century, this static view of history gave way to the dynamics of change. Fatefully, this was the very period in which Jews were at last gaining admission to universities, those essential gateways into modern society. The notion that the "new history" could uncover truth came as an intellectual thunderbolt to the modernizing, emancipated Jews of western and central Europe. Instead of the Talmudic academy's eternal belief that all sacred Jewish texts taught the same lessons, educated people could now understand how Judaism altered with the ages. This insight gave modernizers the authority and self-confidence to seek the Jewish truth that emancipation was opening up to them.

In 1832, this radical approach to classic Jewish texts received a stunning justification. At the instigation of Jewish traditionalists, the German government had ruled that preaching sermons in German—an innovation of some modern synagogues—was illegal since historically, preaching was not understood to be an established Jewish practice. But a young scholar named Leopold Zunz (1794–1886) published a critical, developmental history of the classic books of the midrash. From this data, he was able to demonstrate that Jewish preaching had occurred in rabbinic times and long afterward. Once Zunz had shown how Jews could radically increase their understanding of the Jewish past by reading the data with an evolutionary perspective, the notion of a Judaism that had been relatively unchanged over the millennia lost its credibility.

The power of history interpreted dynamically was finally applied to Jewish belief by the second president of the Hebrew Union College, Kaufmann Kohler (1843–1926). In 1918, this extraordinarily learned scholar published a pioneering work called *Jewish Theology, Systematically and Historically Considered*. Chapter by chapter, he reviewed the spectrum of Jewish affirmations, confidently indicating what each historical period and movement had contributed to a specific topic and concluding with his modern understanding of the belief in question. (Kohler was open minded enough to occasionally discuss Jewish mysticism; but as his view of modernity required, he completely subordinated these ideas to those of modern Jewish philosophy.) An extraordinary student of his times, Kohler stressed each generation's ethical ideas but paid little or no attention to the way Jewish law and practice inculcated Jewish belief. Kohler's historical theology was a masterwork of its day, but it soon became an academic anachronism.

Whereas Zunz, Kohler, and their colleagues had little doubt about how to conduct their craft, today's historians appear to differ, sometimes quite significantly, on what constitutes a proper reading of history. Shall former times be understood from the top down, giving pride of place to leaders and their adversaries? Or shall we approach history from the bottom up, seeing common folk as the true bearers of social destiny? Shall we take for granted the general accuracy of official records, or shall we see them as apologies for those who wrote or sponsored them?

Furthermore, what records shall we include or exclude, and how shall we proceed when there are no direct accounts of what actually took place or had been thought? If we have cited evidence for a certain belief, have we also presented the contrary points of view that Jewish texts often contain? What credence shall we give to different types of evidence, and what value shall we assign to the various kinds of data we retrieve? Perhaps most troubling of all, what concerns does the historian bring to the task, seeing just this but not that, sensitive to some patterns and issues but relatively indifferent to those that another historian would consider critical? These questions are not meant to deny that much can still be learned from the various accepted approaches to uncovering the past. Yet the idea that historical study can uncover the truth about what once happened or was believed has itself become an outdated notion.

It is precisely the truth Jews can believe and build their lives on today that primarily concerns me as I ask what Judaism can teach us. I know I am not creating Judaism afresh, and I do want to know how my Jewish inheritance might still inform the Jewish people. But such openness to the past is not the same as saying that once the teachings of yesteryear have been unearthed, they should dictate our faith today. Historical theology can certainly help us clarify what made our ancestors religiously distinctive and kept their faith alive despite great hardship. But it rarely answers the modern mind's vastly different set of questions about belief raised by contemporary science, psychology, and philosophy. That begins only when every intellectual resource at our disposal is called on and used, responding to what we believe as a result of our fresh exposure to God's Covenant with our people. We surely want God to be our God, yet also the God of our forebears and, we pray, the God of our children and theirs.

38

Jewish God–Talk's Four Criteria

When liberal Jewish thinkers speak about what Jews ought to believe, they have nothing compulsory in mind. Like the Rabbis in the Talmud, the ideas they come up with are not presented as a statement we must affirm to be good Jews. (That, let me hasten to emphasize, holds true for what I've just said and for everything else in this book!) Judaism doesn't focus on required beliefs because the central concern of the Torah is acts, not ideas. So those of us who are devoted to philosophizing about Jewish belief usually keep tabs on our Jewish authenticity by asking how the consequences of these beliefs will fulfill Jewish duty. Let me show how that works when applied to something as theoretical as new ways to think about God. I will limit myself to four critical examples, although others of lesser significance could readily be given.

Perhaps the first, most obvious criterion would require that this new notion of God makes the life of Torah "necessary." Contemplation may expand our spirits, but Torah needs to be *done* continually: The sick need to be visited, people need to gain more learning, and communities need to increase justice and spread compassion. After all, it is not enough that a new God-idea stimulates us to *think* differently about the fundamental Oneness in the universe. An adequate Jewish idea of *Adonai* will move us to do these deeds and others like them. The doing will testify to the way this view of God moves people to work at the Torah's agenda, making God's reality visible in the world.

The more completely a conception of God motivates the performance of Torah—in the evolutionary, creative sense that liberal Jews understand Torah today—the more acceptable that new thinking about God will become. Conversely, if a new vision of God attracts us by its ingenious sophistication but is indifferent to charity, prayer, social action, or other significant aspects of Torah, this talking about God will pain the believing Jewish heart.

Then, too, the life of Torah is not meant to be carried out in isolation, which is why our history mentions relatively few hermits. Rather, the Torah was famously given to a folk, the ethnic group we know as the people of Israel. So a second way to judge the adequacy of Jewish God-talk is to ask if it calls for the continuing existence of the Jewish people. It was God's Torah, not genetics, that transformed the Hebrews into Israel. It was God's Torah, not politics, that fashioned our people's distinctive character. And it was the Jewish people as a whole who pledged their loyalty to God's Covenant, thereby becoming God's people, just as the Eternal One became Israel's God. The Jews exist as Israel because of the unique relationship with God. An understanding of God that negates the people of Israel's pact with God moves outside the sphere of Jewish belief.

A third criterion to judge a fresh depiction of God relates to the many inherited Jewish metaphorical terms for God. Reflecting on the nature of God has taken such diverse paths during the three millennia of recorded Jewish existence that it is most unlikely an innovative sense of God can come to the Jewish community as a complete surprise. In the Bible, God has been variously personified as sculptor, orchardist, warrior, lover, judge, penitent, weeper, lawgiver, laborer, rester, author, general, mother, and much else. In rabbinic times and beyond, these biblical glimpses are creatively surpassed by hints of Jewish mystical views. A plethora of inherited Jewish ways of referring to God certainly need not reiterate what the Jewish imagination produced in ages past. However, if this new example of God-talk radically differs from the flood of images that have come from the Jewish soul in prior times, contemporary Jewry will receive it with considerable suspicion.

Any new characterization of the One "Who has brought us to this day" will also face a fourth test: the promise that this new notion of the Divine will promote the long-range future of Judaism. If our prior history holds, generations long after ours will decide the adequacy of our ideas about God by testing them with the challenges that history will bring their way. A new concept of God will show its ultimate value to our covenanted people through its long-range durability. Future generations will be the final arbiter of the vitality of a once-innovative notion of God. Any thinking that does not encourage the doing of *mitzvot* for the long haul is unworthy of Jewish devotion in the present.

The ultimate judgment, of course, is messianic. Our God needs to lead us to the time when, as the prophet Zechariah so memorably put it, a day arrives when what we call God and what in fact is God prove to be identical (14:9). As believing Jews, we cannot be religiously satisfied with a God-language that does not reach as far as our souls' dearest dream. We surely must keep our messianic aspirations in mind if someone urges us to adopt a new sense of God that would replace our older one. Our messianism will always have an unimpeachable claim on the virtue of any new view of God.

Jewish folklore—no authoritative source but not without its wisdom—tells us that the prophet Elijah will bring answers to all our questions about Jewish religious understanding and ritual obligation when he returns to earth to announce the coming of the Messiah. Until that day, I hope my guidance helps you on your faithful journey.

The Brain–Heart
Interplay in Faith

39

I discovered an important aspect of the Jewish religious duty of study, *talmud torah*, when I taught Jewish thought at secular universities. This certainly wasn't evident on the surface, for we studied the same books with the same critical-appreciative approach that I used with my rabbis- and cantors-to-be at Hebrew Union College–Jewish Institute of Religion. My perplexities finally lifted the year I taught at Harvard's multidenominational Divinity School, where my most perceptive student in Jewish thought was a Christian Palestinian woman. That experience made clear to me that the balance between the brain and the heart was different at the university and the seminary.

I am not implying that secular institutions are entirely cognitive and make no place for intuition. Most university professors of religion want their students to appreciate why people worldwide may find the teachings of religions other than their own attractive. Going further, trying to win student allegiance to a given faith would violate a nondenominational school's commitment to intellectual freedom.

Those who study at the seminary and the synagogue want to do the same intellectual work, yet they also want to fulfill the commandment that follows closely on the prayer at the heart of

Judaism, the Shema: "And these words which I command you this day shall be upon your heart" (Deuteronomy 6:6). Ideally, Jews who seek out Jewish study aspire to more than a few credits on their cultural transcript. They look to Torah as their long-range, motivating truth. Life being complex and hopefully lengthy, they will therefore want to acquire as great a knowledge of Jewish teaching as they possibly can—the lifetime project that comes from loving with all your heart and soul and might. Thus every good Jewish teacher will seek to move through the mind to create an impassioned heart.

But—why is there always a "but"?—a particularly modern problem then confronts us. I don't mean those common inhibitors of religious practice: "I have so many other important things to do"; "Almost no one else I know takes this so seriously"; "It's too complicated, too different, and has too little payoff." No, these and other contemporary alibis for impiety don't get to the nub of the religious brain-heart clash. This arises because most modern scholarship is based on methodological doubt. Scholars these days are always itching to ask "How do you know that?" or "What's the evidence for that?"

What gives such questions about religion their special edge is that the only answers that these academics will accept are secular or "brain centered." Insisting God be sidelined when the issue is factual may not be terribly disturbing: Was the world created fifty-seven-plus centuries ago? Did six hundred thousand Jews leave Egyptian slavery? Did invading Israelites annihilate the Canaanites (per the Book of Joshua) or troublingly live alongside them for generations (per the Book of Judges)? Data occasionally turns up showing that the Bible is more accurate than we thought or that certain scholarly views were overly self-assured. However, in answering such queries by recourse to either midrash (the traditionalists) or to the fallible human authors of the text (the liberals), most Jewish scholarship has conceded skeptics' claims about the dubious factuality of early biblical accounts.

If the Bible doesn't always get its facts right, why should people trust it for what it says about God or people or what God wants people to do? And if we have to bring a healthy skepticism to postbiblical teaching as well, how can we be expected to give this learning our hearts? That's the real brain-heart issue in faith today. It has evoked three main responses: abandon religion; accept that it knows more than we do; make a measure of doubt integral to one's belief.

First, nonbelievers think we will be better off if we give up on religion. Then, when nonbelievers live ethically, they can make a cogent argument for their position. But it isn't clear these days where the ethics come from or at what they aim. In today's varied consumerist culture, the case can be made that worthy nonbelievers are living off the inherited capital of their religious forebears. And anyone, religious or not, who ventures to love surely must have a sense of what it is to live by faith.

Second, traditionalists of all religions believe that given the tawdriness of much modern life, their faith "knows" far more than they do. In Judaism, which effectively has no dogmas or creeds, this thought is reinforced by the tradition's openness in matters of belief and by its acceptance of vigorous debate and different opinions. Here the brain will not lack for exercise as long as the heart leads along the paths of Jewish observance.

Finally, proud as we are of the muscular intellectuality of our spirituality, most caring liberal Jews today believe modernity's truth requires us to be more modest in our faith. Accepting the human role in creating and elaborating on Torah allows for new learning and encourages us to make our own contributions to the dynamic of our faith. This humility enables us to acknowledge the limited vision of prior generations as well as to marvel at their enduring wisdom. Above all, it keeps those with absolute self-confidence from imposing their faith on others, and it encourages liberal believers to challenge the validity of any interpretation of Judaism that violates its fundamental commitment to realizing the Divine potential in everyone.

Because fanaticism and erraticism are such prominent features of religious life in our time, we must not undervalue the brain. But acknowledging that our faith does not know the whole truth makes it all the more critical for the enlightened heart to guide us on our way.

40

Four Ways to Understand "God Says ..."

The Bible seems to have no problems with God's talking to people. In fact, revelation through speech is fairly commonplace. We witness Abraham, Hagar, and other such folks going about their lives when, with little or no warning, God begins to speak to them. Or, uniquely and dramatically, God personally speaks ten instructions to a whole people at Mt. Sinai. Much later, the prophets give their speeches and then laconically add, "That's what God says."

When Jewish thinkers encountered the academic discipline of philosophy in the early Middle Ages, many questions were raised about how this God-human contact was possible. Through the centuries, two issues in particular have evolved regarding revelation. First, we understand that the Divine message conveyed a content that was previously hidden from people; and second, it was hidden because it was a godly truth. With some license, we can say that these assumptions continue to ground our questions about revelation in today's more skeptical, human-centered time.

Four different understandings of revelation currently appeal to most thoughtful Jews.

The first appeals to diverse traditionalists. For the most part, they accept the biblical-rabbinic view of revelation simply because it has been central to Jewish faith for millennia. It, like the very act of

Creation, is one of the many things God does that are beyond human understanding. The philosopher-theologian Abraham Joshua Heschel tried to help skeptical modern Jews find a way to accept this traditional point of view. He felt that what stood in the way was our limited appreciation of God's greatness. His major work on this theme, *God in Search of Man*, highlights the transposition of the common, contemporary view of religion. The book opens with Heschel's exquisitely evocative prose poems, naming six relationships in which moderns might encounter God—the sublime, wonder, mystery, awe, glory, and amazement. Were we more open to God's grandeur, Heschel explains, we could accept God's revealing, even if the biblical accounts of it, as he nicely says, are the midrash, the imaginative interpretation, of this mystery. While *God in Search of Man* remains a classic, Heschel's thinking on this topic is not as influential among liberal Jews—I know of no academic thinker who espouses it—as was his ethical example of marching with Martin Luther King Jr.

Breaking with all God-centric explanations, a second approach to revelation is radically human centered. It seeks to keep religious thinking as rational as possible to connect revelation with human discernment and discovery. The academic version of this position is philosophical, glorying in the way some minds, by insight and precise reasoning, enable us to understand reality and human duty in freshly convincing ways. This more humanistic version is content to know that some people, like Mozart and Einstein, are simply geniuses, able to rise far above what even very bright people can comprehend. Early in our history, the people of Israel had a remarkable run of such religious geniuses—Moses, Deborah, the writers of the Torah, the psalmists, and the prophets—and the world has been their beneficiaries.

The third view bridges the mostly God and mostly human points of view and understands revelation as what occurs in the relationship between people and God. Here the analogy is what, largely wordlessly, passes between those in any significant human relationship. Without ever exhausting the mystery of the partner, a couple continually gain new and deep insight into each other and learn more about who they both are. Something like that takes place between people and God, with the poets and prophets and lawgivers of the Bible putting into language their exceptional sense of the Divine Other with whom Israel stands in Covenant. Many feminist thinkers have found a version of this perspective congenial to their thinking for two reasons: a covenantal relationship emphasizes intimacy, and there is nothing whatsoever in Covenant that suggests a masculine sense of God.

Last, there is the mystic Jewish approach to revelation. What tends to characterize its numerous individualistic forms is the insight that ultimately there is only God, and a gap between the human and the Divine is baseless. We learn this by climbing the experiential ladder, moving from the low level of existence we commonly take to be reality to higher levels of existence, reaching the supreme accomplishment that makes us one with the One. Such religious consummation is rare, even for the geniuses of Jewish mysticism; however, we lesser souls know how much closer to God we may become. This is why the history of Jewish mysticism is one not only of intense piety but of disciplined observance as well.

Many variations of these ideas exist in our community today. The supreme example, common to all Jewish belief, is the veneration of the Torah scroll, the most significant of all our documents of revelation as most liberals understand it. The Torah is our only holy object, the near-at-hand focus of our worship, the object in whose presence we respectfully rise and lovingly kiss. When we recount how we receive Torah, we are in awe—indeed, its Revelation remains the basis of our lives. In sum, our theories of revelation seek to explain why we believe what we believe, and what they do not make plain, our actions seek to complete.

Clarifying Some Feminist Ideas

41

There is so much justice to the claims of feminist thinkers and so vast an agenda of what needs to be done to bring women to full human equality that I hesitate to suggest some modest rethinking of a few otherwise incontrovertible feminist assertions. Having been warned that male assessments of feminine thought are typically viewed as efforts to reassert control, I offer these ideas with considerable hesitancy. Nonetheless, I hope that what I feel needs to be said turns out to be a congenial extension of what women thinkers are themselves seeking.

My thinking about this topic got started as I viewed and later reflected on some films by feminist moviemakers, the most interesting being *Whale Rider* and *Antonia's Line*. Both movies projected a feminist model of small group organization; they emphasized the critical ethical distinction between operating in a typical "masculine-authoritarian" fashion versus following a "feminist-communitarian" style. I think that men as well as women have acknowledged that patriarchal dominance of a group, with its strong, top-down mode of doing things, generally impedes the efforts of trying to achieve full humanity. This feminist critique of our inherited technique for working together has greatly enhanced our vision of what we need to do in order to improve our lives.

I was also moved by the movies' depiction of two subsidiary evils created by patriarchy—otherness and hierarchy. The former subtly distinguishes between the familiar in-group who has the most power and gets the most benefits, and all the rest that are other, excluded from the favored few. Judith Plaskow (b. 1946), the pioneering philosopher of Jewish feminism, gave this memorable example in her feminist classic, *Standing Again at Sinai*. She zeros in on the language used in the Book of Exodus that recounts God's directions to the Hebrews about purifying themselves for the incomparable moment at Mt. Sinai, when God personally told them the ten basic commands that they all were to live by. God says, "Don't go near a woman" (Exodus 19:15). The men were legitimized; the women were merely others. When in all sorts of situations we categorize all sorts of people as "others," we have silently validated the sinful behavior of treating them badly. In our own day, we may talk about the equality of the sexes, but, in fact, we continue to pay women less than men.

A similar instance of negative distinction is hierarchy, the ranking of people with regard to power and its privileges. While there have been modest improvements in this area, women continue to be disproportionately found in the lower echelons of corporate and nonprofit institutions, as well as excluded from most of the higher levels of these same organizations.

These feminist concerns, reminiscent of prophetic calls for greater justice in Jewish life, have revolutionized the way non-Orthodox Jews now think about their social and religious structures. Of course, there is much yet to be done to make them our accepted practice. All that being true, I nonetheless want to suggest that achieving these worthy feminist aims requires a certain measure of these harmful practices.

In both films, the tension of the plots came from the risky effort to move a group from the accepted patriarchal style toward a more communitarian life. Yet I noted that the transition from one to the other was not complete. In these stories, the feminist heroine who instigated the change never became simply another member of her group. She retained a quiet leadership role, one that never reverted to anything like the old authoritarian model, but still gave her a special effectiveness in her group. In the ideal commune, no one has special authority and all group roles are interchangeable. The several efforts to put such absolute equality in practice have proved to be unworkable. Many early kibbutzim (collective settlements) in Israel tried to follow this model, as did American hippy communes of the 1960s. Before long, human nature made these idealistic efforts impractical; truth be told, some people are simply more effective leaders than others.

Something like this is also true about making absolute the threat of otherness. Surely we do not want everyone to be the same, as identical as novelist Ira Levin's *Stepford Wives*. Without some otherness, we could not succeed as individuals, a cherished liberal maxim. In *Whale Rider* and *Antonia's Line*, the women who became catalysts for change did so because their ethical perceptions made them sufficient outsiders who were moved to remedy societal flaws that others did not perceive. Without a certain otherness, there would be neither prophetic vision nor necessary individual initiative.

Let me also suggest that not all hierarchy tends to diminish those on lesser levels. Our parents may see their offspring as children much longer than we think they should. Yet no matter how old or infirm they become, they are always entitled to our respect and care, our repayment of a small measure of what they incomparably did for us. The same is true of our relationship with God, which is, as it were, the greatest example of hierarchy. But note how this absolutely superior Being exercises power: by giving humans the freedom even to say no to God and thereby making them unique among all living creatures. Hierarchy based on genuine love is granted our heartfelt admiration.

This examination of feminist views of otherness and hierarchy seems to lend itself to a concluding observation: There is something about eye-opening ideas that makes us want to extend them way beyond their original relevance. We need to be wary of pushing a good truth too far. I suggest that as ethically persuasive as feminist ideas are, they too have their limits. These limits do not arise because women and men see things differently but because life itself is as particular as it is universal.

42

Jewish Beliefs about Evil

Jewish faith in all historical periods has generally focused on practical notions of what God wants us to do, rather than on theoretical ideals of understanding God. Thus there are considerably more Jewish books on creating proper communities, decent human relations, and ritual than on theodicy, explaining why a good God tolerates evil. Yet through the centuries, reasonably clear if diverse patterns of Jewish beliefs on evil have been identified.

In the **Hebrew Bible,** the story of Creation presents a framework for all that follows. The Genesis narrative emphasizes that God's Creation was good, indeed "very good," which makes the subsequent introduction of evil, the anti-good, a problem. This account is not concerned with natural evils like cancer or tsunamis, but with people's misuse of their freedom. God responds to both human righteousness and sin with a Divine system of justice, rewarding goodness and punishing bad human behavior. A secondary strand of the Bible's basic understanding of evil treats it as God's pedagogy. God respects human freedom but at the same time teaches people how to do the good. Other biblical writers declare that since God micromanages the universe, natural evils are God's doing as well.

There are three biblical points of view that counter this God-driven theory of evil. First, the Book of Psalms in particular is filled with complaints by people who cry against God's system of justice. They say that it doesn't operate in a timely fashion and thus is guilty of creating evil itself! Second, when Job charges that the system doesn't work at all, God, in effect, responds by saying, "You couldn't understand it even if I tried to explain it to you," which becomes the classic Jewish explanation of evil. The third motif, rarely mentioned in the Bible but featured in medieval Jewish mysticism, is the snake that tempted Eve. That is, an evil force was built into Creation itself! But if Creation was so good, why is this tempter needed?

The teachers of the **Rabbinic Period,** roughly from 100 BCE to about 1000 CE, stress the merits of the Divine system of justice, often to show how effectively that system can work. The Rabbis portray humans as conflicted by good and evil urges, noting that as long as a person lives, the evil urge is unremitting and can be only temporarily outwitted.

However, the Rabbis resolve a basic problem with the biblical justice system by extending its effect beyond history. Their eschatology, their theological concerns with the end of days, pivots around a resurrection of the dead that is followed by God's judgment on individuals and communities, and the subsequent meting out of appropriate rewards and punishments. Despite modern howls about the inconsistency of greatly delayed justice, this remains the accepted belief of observant Orthodox Jews and even some liberal Jews today.

Two major interpretations of these beliefs arose in the **Middle Ages** (around 1000 to 1800 CE), one philosophical and the other mystical. Notwithstanding their fundamental differences, both approaches resolve the problem of evil by envisioning it as the consequence of a faulty attitude. Philosophers taught that evil was not in fact real but merely the absence of good. Though this theory solved the logical challenge of locating non-good in a good God's world, it never gained much popular acceptance in the oft-suffering Jewish community.

Mystics and kabbalists took evil much more seriously. Their doctrine holds that God exists as ten good nodes or s'firot of diverse energy that were then paired with ten evil s'firot. The mystics' climactic response taught that evil is only an illusion. In fact, there are four levels of reality: *atzilah*, emanation; *beriyah*, creation; *yetzirah*, forming; and *asiyah*, making. Alas, we reside on the lowest level, where evil is rampant. However, it is possible for us to rise to a higher level through mystic exercises. Then we will leave spurious individuality and its evils behind, and identify and ultimately become one with the only Reality, the one, good God.

For all intents and purposes, human reason in the **Modern Period** (ca. 1800–ca. 1970) took the place of God, and agnosticism reigned in modernized Jewish communities. Scientific minds rejected the problem of trying to defend God's goodness, and Jewish belief was seen as focusing on the ethics generated by the rational mind, with its goal of bringing on a humanly created messianic order.

The Holocaust, followed by totally new postmodern intellectual philosophies, largely destroyed this optimistic vision of humankind. What, then, could ground our values? The answer—a considerable turn to religious belief in Judaism, as in other faiths.

The few remaining Jewish rationalists now assert that God is good and real but limited in power. Far more widespread is the non-rational notion that religious belief needs to be seen as a relationship rather than as a way of thinking. According to this view, if the relationship is to remain solid, we must remain lovingly involved even though we can't always understand God. Contemporary Jewish mystics reassert the old kabbalistic insight that we need to rise to a higher level of consciousness to be rid of evil. Jewish feminist theologians largely confine their contribution to this topic by calling attention to the special evils of sexism and patriarchy.

Together with Orthodoxy and its reinterpretations of classic Jewish ideas, these seem to be the major contemporary Jewish religious approaches to evil. None dominates Jewish belief today. Yet in some way that surpasses our understanding, despite our harsh experience of evil, most Jews remain inordinately committed to struggling for the good.

43

The Messianic Hope Today

It may be reckless, but I propose to identify the main theme of the Bible: God's problem of convincing humanity to unreservedly and regularly do God's will. Many people are quite surprised that politics plays a central role in this contentious God-human interaction. While other religions focus on the individual, the central concerns of the Hebrew Bible, beginning in the Book of Exodus, are the difficulties of sanctifying national power. To put it another way, how does a sovereign nation-state, an institution with almost unlimited power, freely do God's bidding?

Moses confronts this issue in much of the Torah, and the historical books of the Bible are obsessed with it. See 1 Samuel 8 with its sad reactions to the Hebrews' request for a human sovereign, God having been their *melech* (King) until that point. The rest of the prophets then inveigh on little else. Yes, the books in the third section of the Hebrew Bible, the part called "The Writings," are often more individualistic; most of Psalms and all of Job and Ecclesiastes testify to this. Nonetheless, the preoccupation with sanctifying communal power reasserts itself in the narrative books of Esther, Daniel, Ezra, Nehemiah, and both Chronicles, as well as in some of the poetry of Psalms and all of Lamentations.

I am continually awed by the religious realism of our ancestors in seeking to sanctify group power. Getting individuals to become more righteous is certainly no small challenge, as most of our own lives indicate. But getting governments (and highly placed individuals in governments) to overcome the corruption that power induces calls for outwitting the safeguards of eternal vigilance as well as checks and balances. When we attempt to turn a divine dream into a societal reality—a time when "nations stop [even] studying about war" (Isaiah 2:4 and Micah 4:3), and everyone "can sit under a vine and fig tree and no one makes them afraid" (Micah 4:4)—we begin to sense the expansive horizon of Jewish faith.

Non-Orthodox scholars of the Hebrew Bible, Christian as well as Jewish, believe that allusions in the Bible to this God-oriented, human-fulfilling time are wonderful, but they are essentially natural reactions to bad kings or disappointing times. These scholars point to a number of passages that foresee such an era yet mention no ideal ruler, arguing that such prophecies are not "messianic" in the end-of-history sense, which clearly arises much later, in pre-rabbinic times.

Whatever the historical development of the Messiah idea, its logic is reasonably constant: If one good God controls the universe, God's purpose in history will not ultimately be defeated. Rather, "it will come to pass in the end of days" (Isaiah 2:1 and Micah 4:1). If the major impediment to governments that do God's will is bad rulers, then one day there will be a Sovereign who is so filled with God's spirit that his or her justice will be perfect and her or his reign will be thoroughly beneficent. Note the partnership motif in this notion. The Ruler Messiah does not accomplish the task by personal cleverness in political science or practical politics; God's help is needed in both areas. For God's part, God, the Covenanter, imbues this special human agent with the wisdom and divine purpose to carry it out.

While some rabbis, in their typically hyperbolic preaching, insist that Israel or God might bring about this historic consummation without assistance, partnership is the more common means. What-ever the overwhelming problem, God and people will eventually overcome it. Since the Rabbis never agreed on a single narrative for the advent of God's ultimate triumph, we have to imaginatively reconstruct its various stages. The messianic drama begins with a grievous period of war and suffering; the Jewish people finally tri-umphs; the prophet Elijah comes to answer all questions and to announce the coming of God's Chosen. This Ruler-Messiah then establishes peace and plenty; the graves open and the dead are res-urrected. Individuals and nations are judged, with some doomed to destruction while others undergo a limited, purgative punishment. Survivors enter life eternal and join the righteous in the healing and fulfillment of God's presence.

Over the centuries, in many folkloric variations, this brand of messianism sustained and empowered Jewish devotion. This changed in the nineteenth century, as western-European Jews had the mes-sianic experience of becoming equals in their secular societies—emancipations due to political change, not God's intervention. As a result, most modernizing Jews came to believe that good politics was the most effective means of radically improving the world. This modernistic Jewish optimism about what the human could and would likely soon accomplish made belief in the Divinely inspired Ruler-Messiah untenable. However, it left the messianic goal intact for political idealists, many of whom were Jewish: communists, socialists, anarchists, Zionists, and others who fervently promoted their theories as the surest path to reach the messianic age.

Alas, history has cruelly disabused us of our optimism about human nature and the wisdom of relying on human power alone to transform history. We surely need God's help to mend the world's ills. That does not mean we have become passive in the face of human injustice. Indeed, most of us believe it a grievous sin not to exercise the power that we may have in order to reduce suffering and increase well-being. Seeing ourselves as God's partners in this grand enterprise, we do not find the image of God's anointed, the Messiah, to be a fitting symbol for our grandest hope in history.

With the wisdom that our working and waiting relies as much on God's doing as upon our own, I find the idea of the messianic age a fitting vision to spur my will and enlarge my soul.

44

Life after Death

I almost never quote myself, but I once gave what I still think is good advice about this tough topic, and I think it's worth repeating.

> Don't try to imagine what it is like being dead ... whatever
> you come up with has to be awful. Death being the oppo-
> site of life ... all you can imagine is different kinds of noth-
> ingness. The point is, however, you won't "be" dead. Think
> about it: being dead means "you" are dead and you won't
> "be" or "feel" anything, not even bad. The words "being"
> and "dead" make no sense together. If you have "being,"
> you're not "dead." Either there is some sort of life after
> death and "being dead" refers to what you're doing in that
> existence, or else you're dead, in which case "you" won't
> know it.
>
> Eugene Borowitz, *Liberal Judaism*, 1984, page 210

So the first thing is to stop trying to figure out what it is like to be no-thing.

The nub of our problem is that we moderns insist on understanding things based on our personal experience. What can we sensibly say about something we've never experienced, namely, death and what comes afterward? In contrast, though it's not easy talking about God, at least we can refer to those moments when we've had the feeling that God is real, even near. With death, the closest most of us have ever felt to it is sleep, which is only a different kind of consciousness. We just have nothing to compare death to; death is a real mystery to us—and a scary one at that.

Probing a bit further, I think we can turn up some personal experiences that aren't directly about life after death, but nonetheless suggest its reality to believing Jews. This is particularly so because Jewish tradition has made us aware of and responsive to God's creativity. Let me take myself as an example. Though I know that my "self" is intricately related to my body and its ingenious processes, I also know myself to be fundamentally a person, not merely a chemical compound like an aspirin. One good reason I feel this way is that I can appreciate the God who daily showers goodness upon me and everyone else—I'm blessed that my religious faith keeps me open to the endless possibility of life's wonders.

I also know something about God and what God wants of me. At my best, my actions help to complete God's work of Creation. This exalted human capacity surely deserves as much respect as does our chemistry, for it is precisely our "God-helping" that makes us characteristically human. These feelings are the experiential base of my Jewish intuition that I am created "in God's image," the old sense that people are somehow "like" God.

The more we make our lives correspond to what we share in the reality of God's eternal presence, the more we may trust that even beyond the grave we can share in God's eternal life. We hope to do that personally, since our individuality is founded on God's own singleness. Thus I join with all those Jews over the ages who have fervently hoped that God will honor our individuality by granting us some type of personal survival after death.

All this I can say without hesitation; however, I am ambivalent about another contemporary reason offered for believing in an afterlife—the near-death experiences reported by people who were clinically dead and later shocked back into life. A significant proportion of them report undergoing certain similar transitional events. More telling, I think, is their later accurate recounting of what was going on around them when they were medically dead. But all this, as opposed to what others who have undergone resuscitation and experienced nothing, seems to be sufficiently ambiguous that I am loathe to base my faith on it.

Yet I do find some corroborative value in the practical effects of affirming life after death. Believing as a liberal Jew in humankind's significant role as God's partner, I am unlikely to believe in what the Depression-era leftist critics of religion decided was a "pie in the sky by and by" afterlife, that is, one that makes us passive to the world's continuing injustice. I admit that because I don't think people are exclusive agents in the messianic project—God is helping us—I don't invest every immediate social struggle with ultimate messianic urgency. Should this or that project fail to advance the coming of God's rule, I will not be as dispirited as some who cannot bear it when their activities fail to usher in even a sample of the messianic age. Believers who do not expect vindication in this life alone are not personally defeated when humanity proves obstinate to change or malevolent in intent. They trust that God will not be defeated in history and that they will be rewarded in another existence. And that emboldens them, even though they suffer for God's sake in this world.

I confess I don't know how I shall survive, what sort of judgment awaits me, or what I shall do in eternity. I am inclined to think that my hope is better spoken of as a resurrection rather than as immortality. I feel too "embodied" to seriously consider myself a soul without a body, though I have no idea what sort of body God will contrive for me after the grave. Resurrection may be too strong a claim for me to make on my own; I incline toward it because the Jewish tradition, which otherwise so powerfully shapes my being, so strongly affirms it.

Ultimately, I trust in what I have experienced of God's overwhelming generosity, which has manifested itself so often in my life. That often enables me to wholeheartedly sing out the last stanza of "*Adon Olam*": "In God's hand I place my soul, both when I sleep and when I wake, and with my soul, my body. God is with me. I shall not fear."

VI
Learning from Holy Thinkers

45

Why I Am a Theologian Rather than a Philosopher

Enough people have been puzzled by my calling myself a theologian rather than a philosopher, the more common Jewish term for a religious thinker, that a few words about that seem warranted. (Mentally I add the question, "And does that make any real difference to people who read or listen to me?") I guess things are so terminologically loose these days that bothering about what anyone calls my kind of thinking seems pretty pedantic. But something useful can be learned about Jewish belief by exploring the difference between these overlapping but diverse ways of looking at reality.

Some brief explanations should clarify things. Theologians start their thinking from their belief in a given faith; how extensive that initial commitment is will vary with the faith and the thinker involved. By contrast, ever since René Descartes (1596–1650; "I think, therefore I am"), philosophers have used methodical doubt to clear their minds of everything but the logic of thinking and its consequences. This being the root difference between Jewish philosophers and Jewish theologians, it wasn't uncommon a few decades back for philosophers to attack theologians as having closed minds, while philosophers celebrated their own open-mindedness, hardly the kind of judgment you'd expect from a truly open-minded person!

As Jews emerged into the modern world during the nineteenth century and their approaches to knowledge were shaped by the university, they quickly gave up their old textual forms of reasoning for the then-current philosophical ways of thinking. Two major factors impelled this development. First, the greatest universities of that time were located in Germany, and philosophy was considered their chief glory. So even the majority of Jews who did not specialize in philosophy began to speak in the styles of the philosophers Immanuel Kant or Georg Wilhelm Friedrich Hegel or one of their numerous German successors. Second, modernizing Jews were desperately eager to prove that they were just like everyone else, and philosophy focused on the truths that all rational minds should share, producing an invigorating climate for those seeking to shed their old Jewish baggage.

A famous squabble later broke out between some Jews who were so eager to be considered modern Germans that they spurned their ethnicity, becoming enthusiastic devotees of philosophy's openness, and some eastern-European Jewish nationalists who conceived of Judaism as an independent source of value and truth, thus thinking in terms of Jewish philosophy. It was a futile hope for the latter group. This was made clear by the title of Hermann Cohen's 1919 book, *Religion of Reason out of the Sources of Judaism*, which once and for all established the academic validity of philosophizing about Judaism. Cohen's philosophy, neo-Kantianism (a revision of Kant's thought that restored its academic legitimacy), first establishes what any rational mind should arrive at: religion of reason. Then, if we look at the many religions created over the centuries, we will find from the "sources of Judaism" that the Jewish religion, as Cohen interprets it, exemplifies religion of reason uniquely well. Though the boundaries have loosened since Cohen wrote, his thesis pretty much describes what the many fine academic philosophers who now write about Judaism try to do: first provide a philosophic truth and then give this concept its Jewish identity. Ironically, today we have relaxed enough to call this enterprise Jewish philosophy.

In the 1970s, when American colleges were becoming hospitable to the notion of academic Jewish studies, the old argument over parochialism was reborn. While it may sound self-defeating, it was the Jewish professors who fought the introduction of such courses on many campuses. Some had come to university life to escape their Jewish origins and devote themselves to universal culture. They vigorously opposed programs that might remind people of Jewish particularity. Other professors who were fervent Jewish secularists did support courses in Jewish culture but opposed those that might teach about the Jewish religious tradition. They argued that because religion rests on belief and often seeks converts, it has no place in an academic life that exalts open-mindedness. While these professors are now the exceptions, there are still a few American universities where Jewish studies departments exclude courses based on Judaism as a religion.

My chief encounter with this problem came in 1962, when my article in *Commentary* magazine on the need for Jewish theology was severely criticized as seeking to introduce dogma into Judaism. The criticism ended when I countered that while practice was traditionally required in Judaism, belief was largely a realm of personal judgment. What modern Jewry needed, I contended, was to pay more attention to what we believe and why we held those beliefs. My challenger illustrated the problems that philosophy increasingly came upon as the twentieth century moved forward. His own brilliant skepticism kept him from ever making a major positive statement about the values a rational person should hold.

I could not have imagined then that succeeding decades would validate my youthful insight: Thoughtfully examined belief, i.e. "theology," would become an important ingredient in the spiritual life of American Jewry. That happened because with the passage of time, it became increasingly apparent that the vaunted objectivity of modern philosophy was actually founded on some fairly subjective assumptions—cultural, political, racial, and sexist. Moreover,

Jewish philosophers learned the impossibility of thinking without specific content in mind. One must have a sense of something in order to begin to think. With philosophy itself transformed, it did not seem unreasonable to suggest that religious belief might also involve quite deep thinking, though not always in the forms pioneered for us by the great Greek philosophers.

As I see it, contemporary Jewish theology often centers on clarifying the balance in our faith between belief and reasoning; those of us who refer to ourselves as Jewish theologians will emphasize one or another as we believe Jewish truth requires. Only future generations of Jewish believers will be able to judge which statements best explained what Torah meant in our times.

Seven People Who Shaped Modern Jewish Thought

46

In describing the main currents of non-Orthodox Jewish belief, seven authors in particular (though there are, of course, others) reshaped how Judaism is thought about and continue to stimulate contemporary discussion. From 1919 to 1956, Hermann Cohen, Mordecai Kaplan, Franz Rosenzweig, Martin Buber, and Abraham Joshua Heschel created intellectual patterns that still influence us. In 1990 and 1997, respectively, Judith Plaskow and Rachel Adler transformed all of our theological thinking.

All of these founding intellectuals combined rationality and experience; however, just how they understood and correlated them gives their takes on Judaism their special character. Here is a brief summary of their positions.

Hermann Cohen (1842–1918) and Mordecai Kaplan (1881–1983) insisted (somewhat differently, to be sure) that we should only believe ideas our minds found convincing and the duties these ideas authorized, primarily ethics. Cohen had an international reputation for his ingenious renewal of the great eighteenth-century thinker Immanuel Kant's philosophy. Kant's intellectual system asserts that reason operates in three diverse modes—scientific, ethical, and aesthetic—but since we have primary evidence that our minds think as a unity, we need to add a foundational, unifying concept to our thinking. Cohen's basic, integrating idea identified what religions had crudely intuited as "God." This academic, secular understanding of how a rational, modern mind functions was the criterion for what Cohen called humankind's "religion of reason," the human ideal. Cohen argued that this validated Judaism because, of all religions, it came closest to being a religion of reason. This is due to Judaism's emphasis on God's uniqueness and on the moral law that is the heart of its notion of mitzvah (commandment). Cohen's high standard set the intellectual level for all the thinkers who, in their own distinctive ways, took up his tasks.

A generation later, Mordecai Kaplan, who served as a congregational rabbi in the United States and who also taught at The Jewish Theological Seminary of America, agreed that to be modern, a Jew needed to think rationally, although he rejected philosophy as the best model for doing so. Writing in the heyday of the American fascination with science, Kaplan wanted Jews to use a scientific model to shape their Judaism. Critical of Cohen for effectively leaving Jewish peoplehood out of his thought, Kaplan based his image of Judaism on the emerging scientific discipline of sociology. This ingeniously enabled him to reverse the normal structure of traditional Jewish belief. Instead of the classical vision of God giving Torah and thus endowing Jews with a special way of life, Kaplan argued sociologically and inverted the process. He saw the Jewish people, like all peoples, creating a multifaceted culture, or "civilization," that among other things included a religion which evolved a distinctive idea of God. He was rationalistic enough to give a definition of God, the only Jewish thinker to ever do this. Kaplan's God is "The Power [or our unifying image of all those forces in nature] that makes for salvation [or human fulfillment]."

Today's Jewish thinkers who work from a contemporary philosophy are Cohen's intellectual descendants, while those who employ grand scientific theories like evolution or cosmology are, for all the substantial differences from sociology, Kaplan's intellectual offspring.

Two German thinkers from the post–World War I turmoil in European thought, Martin Buber (1878–1965) and Franz Rosenzweig (1886–1929), were part of the widespread rejection of the notion that human beings are primarily rational. They helped put forward the view that being a person involves much more than being logical. The mind needs to build from experience, specifically the experience of having a relationship. Thus, while love shouldn't be mindless, we simply can't think our way into love; and love, as Judaism's central prayer, the Shema, makes plain, is the ideal Jewish way of relating to God. Buber subtly but poetically clarified what is and what isn't a true personal relationship and how relationship engenders duty—not only a personal but also a people's connection to God.

Rosenzweig, taking a more cosmic approach to human existence, asserted that we all face three primary, independent realities: God, people (he preferred "man"), and the world. The dynamic relationships between them yielded Judaism's three fundamental religious themes: God relates to the world via creation and to people via revelation, while people relate to the world via redemption. Today's Jewish thinkers who speak in various ways of our relationship with God—like most feminists—follow the Buber-Rosenzweig lead.

Abraham Joshua Heschel (1907–1972), a Pole, was one of the youngest in a group of European scholars brought to the United States in 1939 by the Hebrew Union College; he later taught at the Jewish Theological Seminary. In the 1950s, he established himself as the proponent of a major new way of thinking about Jewish religious experience. With his extraordinarily evocative statement of where we moderns might meet God, Heschel moved far beyond Buber's and Rosenzweig's notion of humans as active partners in our relationship with the Eternal One. Rather, Heschel argued, if we are truly in relationship with *Adonai*, we will let God be God and accept the miracle that God, as the Bible says, revealed Torah to us. In his later writing, Heschel went on to emphasize the strong ethical implications of biblical revelation and gave it iconic exemplification by marching with Dr. Martin Luther King Jr. in the civil rights struggle. While Heschel remains an inspiration and challenge to contemporary thinking about God, revelation, and ethics, his traditionalistic, God-centered reconciliation of them has found few followers.

For some decades these systems dominated American Jewish thought, until Jewish feminist theology emerged and Judith Plaskow issued its fundamental statement. With prophetic indignation, she reminded a Jewish community that prided itself on its ethical commitment how it was nonetheless perpetuating a broad-ranging, patriarchal deprecation of women. Plaskow applied this denunciation of patriarchy to the Bible's depiction of God and of "the Jews" as primarily its males. She looked positively to the untapped resource of feminine experience and put forward a more fully human appreciation of God and our Jewish duty. Among other ideas, Plaskow began to use feminist metaphors for God and adopted a more flexible understanding of human sexuality.

Some years later, after a number of evocative articles, Rachel Adler gave us a full-scale statement of the ways in which the traditions of Jewish obligation might undergo feminist transformation. Seeking a properly feminist praxis—a proactive sense of duty imbued by and closely expressive of our belief—she exposed how the *ketubah*, the classic Jewish marriage contract, gives a patriarchal structure to Jewish marriage. This led to her proposal for a legally authentic and egalitarian substitute for the traditional *ketubah*. Jewish feminism has stimulated a multidirectional outpouring of energy and innovation in North American Jewish life, and much is yet expected from its adherents.

This is a lively time for Jewish religious thought, for many thinkers are presenting promising points of view to the community. There is no way to know which of these will prove significant to the religious life of the Jewish community or the challenges of a dynamic general culture. But there is every reason to hope that with these seven thinkers serving as the foundation of the Jewish intellectual future, we are well equipped to build a rich Jewish spirituality.

Rationalist Thinkers and What They Can Teach Us

47

My thinking has followed a different path from Hermann Cohen's (1842–1918) and Mordecai Kaplan's (1881–1983), Judaism's founding rationalist thinkers, yet I have learned much from each of them and believe their ideas are worthy of examination.

Cohen and Kaplan were not the first modern Jews who sought to explain and validate Jewish belief to their contemporaries. Cohen, however, was the first to write about Judaism on the highest level of contemporary intellectuality; he set the standard for anyone who would later seriously seek to explain the nature of Judaism. Moreover, Cohen's fusion of classic Jewish teaching and modern reasoning continues to influence the content of our Judaism, even though few today think in Cohenian terms. A generation later, Kaplan, a far less innovative thinker, nonetheless importantly demonstrated how Jewish rationalism might mend its flaws, were it recast in terms of the American philosophic idiom of his day—scientific thinking.

As mentioned in chapter 46, Cohen's international fame came from his revival of the thought of the noted late eighteenth-century philosopher Immanuel Kant. The philosophic world had been shaken by a searching question: What really connected our ideas of things to the things themselves? Kant had to admit he couldn't give a rationally valid answer, but he then proposed that we should at least be rational about how our minds worked, to gain knowledge of the things themselves. Later philosophers insisted this analysis might tell us how the mind works but didn't offer any connection to the world itself. Cohen resolved this issue by suggesting that rational thinking is a dynamic through which we seek to create more logical structures that aid our understanding of what we experience as the world itself.

You will note that there is nothing inherently Jewish about Cohen's philosophy. He certainly did not teach Jewish studies at the University of Marburg in Germany; there was no such thing in the late-nineteenth century. Cohen's fame arose from his general philosophic attainment. It was only when anti-Semites began attacking the Jews as an intellectual danger to Germanhood that Cohen began writing essays defending Judaism. Toward the end of World War I, as a retired professor then lecturing at the school for liberal rabbis, Cohen finally put his thinking about Judaism into a book—essentially his class notes that were tidied up for publication by a visiting student named Franz Rosenzweig, who later created a unique way of thinking about Judaism that still intrigues students of Judaism.

Aside from the intellectual eminence that Cohen brought to his exposition of Judaism, there were several important validations of Judaism that emerged from Cohen's work. Chief of these was his assertion that of all the religions in history, Judaism came closest to embodying a "religion of reason," the ethical monotheism suggested by Cohen's secular philosophy. Moreover, since every rational mind needed to be centrally concerned with ethics, Judaism's concentration on deed rather than creed not only made its demands significantly rational, but also provided a criterion by which Jews could now judge which parts of Torah were still valid in modern times. And although Baruch Spinoza, the seventeenth-century Dutch genius who shaped modern philosophy, and the late-eighteenth-century German philosopher Moses Mendelssohn had described Judaism as a religion of law—allowing the German Protestant clergy to disparage Judaism by contrasting our faith to their "religion of love"—Cohen insisted that ethics as a rational discipline must take the form of moral law.

Cohen's ethics-centered Judaism with its aesthetic-oriented worship legitimized post-ghetto Jewish existence. However, its reliance on what every thinking human being should know raised a critical question: Why did we need to be Jewish and not simply good human beings? That was the question that Mordecai Kaplan sought to answer as the twentieth century continued.

Consider Kaplan's time frame. After 1924, mass immigration ended in the United States, due to a law strictly limiting it, particularly that from the "less desirable" southern- and eastern-European countries. As American Jews increasingly acculturated, they came to believe with other Americans that human development would take place as science naturally progressed. Since most of American-schooled Jewry increasingly identified with religious skepticism, Kaplan had the brilliant idea of giving them an interpretation of Judaism that was scientific. This, in accordance with the needs of the time, would make Judaism rational. Moreover, by modeling his theory in terms of the science of sociology, his philosophy would center on the role of the group in the life of an individual.

In the 1930s, when Kaplan began putting forward his ideas, sociology was a relatively young discipline. It taught that the group, not the individual, was primary and that a person's culture (often called "civilization" in Kaplan's day) substantially shaped our individuality. Suddenly land, language, history, art, music, lore, and many other similar concerns became primary factors in Jewish life. Religion, of course, had a significant place in Kaplan's scheme, but Jewish civilization in its broadest sense, not religion, was critical to his Jewishness. Likewise, customs replaced commandments, and God became nature's way of promoting human fulfillment. For a time, when confidence in human progress was high and the regard for abstract philosophy was low, Kaplan's rationalism seemed to be a semisecular, semibelieving community's true salvation.

In subsequent decades, both Cohen's and Kaplan's versions of rationalism have become minority positions in American Jewish life. Today philosophy is not held in high esteem, and solid reasoning seems of limited value in significant human affairs. Yes, we may be less philosophical than other generations, but sometimes we want to think hard about what our faith and our ethics properly demand of us. I and others would not be the Jews we are if we had not been blessed with such good teachers.

Two Misunderstood Messages of Martin Buber

48

Having long championed the esteemed twentieth-century philosopher Martin Buber, I have been challenged over the years with numerous critiques of his work. Two of the most fundamental ones—his radical individualism and his minimal Jewish concern—seem to stem from a fundamental misreading of his classic book *I and Thou*. I believe these critics have missed something in Buber's magnum opus and that their first mistake has led to their second one.

Buber is famous for asserting that someone's "I" (his or her "self") is always involved with an other, which occurs dynamically in two kinds of relationship. He terms the analytic, observational one "I-it," our usual approach to the world. The other, the engaged, involved relationship, he calls "I-thou." There surely is a lot of emphasis on the "I" in this. Please note, however, that Buber says the "I" is always involved with something other than itself, quite different from earlier German philosophers, who made the "I" on its own the source of all understanding.

Buber teaches that all authentic human responsibility comes from the exchange involved in I-thou relationships. These exchanges may be quite slight, as when a person has a casual encounter at the office water cooler or at the reception following

Friday-evening services. These meetings are unlikely to generate more duty than to say a pleasant hello the next time your paths cross. But others may be quite compelling, as is the responsibility that arises from loving someone or the deep sense of involvement with God. Almost everyone who has had a caring family, a good friend, or a special love will testify that this relationship somehow requires us to not just "feel" how close we are, but to show those we love how much we care. This isn't limited to the beloved but affects the way we need to behave when away from our adored ones. Failing to do so damages our relationship, requiring us to make amends for our failings. And all this holds true, remarkably enough, even if our obligation is never put into words; if we really care for another, we should know what we need to do!

What troubles Buber's critics is not his notion that relationship generates duty but his further double insistence about it. For Buber says, if you do not find yourself moved at the particular moment by the I-thou relationship, you are not truly obligated to do something for the other person, even if it's your beloved's birthday! Even if you know you care, what you do about it (buying an elegant cake or beautiful piece of jewelry) is a cultural matter, totally up to each person. So the charge of exaggerated individualism was leveled against Buber.

Two things, I suggest, mitigate the seriousness of this critique. The first, how Buber actually lived his philosophy, makes the charge counterintuitive. He definitely was not someone who spent his years wrapped up in himself. At the turn of the twentieth century, long before most Jewish intellectuals were involved in Zionism, Buber was a passionate advocate for the revival of Jewish folk existence. He served as the first editor of the magazine of the World Zionist Organization, which was founded by the Zionist pioneer Theodor Herzl in 1896. In the 1920s, Buber was one of the leaders of the German interfaith religious socialist movement. A decade later, when Buber finally realized that he needed to leave Germany, he did not settle in another culturally advanced European country. He went instead to the growing community of what was then known as Palestine, before the founding of the modern Jewish state of Israel, to take part in the Jewish people's revival. There he and his followers founded a political party established on the I-thou notion that there should be a binational state comprised of both Arabs and Jews. Thus Buber's record firmly contradicts the accusation that he was a radical individualist.

Second, I contend that Buber's antagonists have overlooked his teaching that groups as well as individuals can have I-thou relationships. Perhaps the clearest example in recent American history has been the civil rights movement of the 1960s. This country was brought together to change its way of thinking and acting through years of nonviolent activism, which climaxed in the march from Montgomery to Selma, Alabama, and in Martin Luther King Jr.'s "I have a dream" speech in front of the Lincoln Memorial in Washington, D.C. Though Buber would reject the language and its implication, Americans became involved in a "we [white Americans]- thou [black Americans]" relationship that altered our sense of social responsibility. This doesn't mean that everyone who was white felt this new empathy for black Americans or had a permanent change of heart. Yet enough of us experienced a new relationship between black and white, and white and black that, despite continuing difficulties, took hold and continues to this day.

Something similar happened to the American Jewish community as a result of the 1967 Six-Day War. The terrible threat of a news blackout for the first three days finally gave way to news of the extraordinary Israeli victory and the Jewish return to Jerusalem's Old City. What had been tepid concern for the newly founded State of Israel by most of the American Jewish community suddenly became an intense involvement in the Jewish people's mutual fate. The Jewish "we-thou" has since asserted itself in ways that have been maintained despite the strains of recent years.

Buber's theoretical writing largely focused on how this folk phenomenon had manifested itself in the early days of recorded history. As the Bible relates, the peoples who experienced a communal I-thou with God and were able to renew that relationship over a period of time created exceptional civilizations and made their marks on human history.

Although secular historians read the Bible with I-it eyes, and therefore could not see how God might be a factor in Jewish (and human) history, Buber brought his I-thou–"we-thou" sensibility to various biblical accounts of the Jewish people and our encounters with God. Reading the narrative that described what happened at Mt. Sinai, Buber could sense the relationship and responsibility that the escaping ex-slaves now experienced in their momentous days at the mountain. True, again and again—as is so typical of human relationships—the people failed to live up to what they had come to know and had pledged themselves to obey. But the Golden Calf episode and the betrayals that followed were overcome by moments as dramatic as Elijah's facing off against the 450 prophets of Baal at Mt. Carmel (1 Kings 18) and the individual preaching of prophets who called for a return to God and Covenant. The Bible, says Buber, is the incomparable record of the Jewish people's perilous establishment of a permanent relationship between countless generations of our people and the One God of the universe.

I do not imagine that this reading of Martin Buber's multileveled understanding of what it means to be involved with God will answer all of the questions that critics have expressed. At least it may show how, despite Buber's great concern for the individual, he was equally concerned for humankind's social existence and the incomparable historic relationship between the Jewish people and God.

Mordecai Kaplan: Ethnicity in Modern Judaism

49

I cannot think of another major book in modern Jewish thought about which I feel as ambivalent as I do toward Mordecai Kaplan's masterwork of 1934, *Judaism as a Civilization*. It is true that some books I once thought wondrously informative, even inspiring, have simply lost their power to stimulate and inform. Kaplan's work, seventy-some years after its appearance, still shoots sparks of insight, but its central thesis has become much less persuasive.

Is it uncharitable of me to complain about a book that has, these decades later, turned out to be quite wrong about the best way for us American Jews to understand ourselves and organize our lives? Books a mere decade older by Franz Rosenzweig and Martin Buber speak more directly to the heart of our community, as does Hermann Cohen's to philosophic academics. However, since individual statements that Kaplan made in this work describe some aspects of Jewish life with a certain wisdom, and since his book has sparked the establishment of the Reconstructionist stream of Judaism, a significant movement in contemporary Jewish life, should I not be more reverential to it? Thus my ambivalence.

Early in *Judaism as a Civilization*, Kaplan gives a strong and not unfair critique of what he saw as the inadequacy of the Reform and Conservative movements to meet the needs of the American Jewish community. To an extent, the leaders of these groups were conscious of the same problems, as their actions in the next decade or so indicated. But more troublesome, I believe, was Kaplan's silence about what he owed to both movements and took for granted in his analysis of the American Jewish experience. Kaplan had originally been an Orthodox rabbi, but the evolutionary attitude he brought to the history of Jewish practice and doctrine was not one he gained from Orthodoxy. His enthusiastic endorsement of Jewish change was substantially learned from the generations of Reform and Conservative thinkers who had preceded him, and his stance as a thinker owed much to them. Kaplan should have forthrightly acknowledged this.

Intellectually, it is still admirable to read Kaplan's insistence that American Jewry's self-understanding ought to be based not on philosophy but on science and its ethics. Despite the economic uncertainties of the Great Depression, great insights were coming from laboratories and researchers, while religion seemed story bound and not a little superstitious. Breaking with the German philosophic bent of an older liberal Judaism, Kaplan boldly called for a shift to naturalism, the American style of philosophizing in a scientific mode. His break with the liberal past took not only great courage but also considerable imagination. Alas, of all the sciences Kaplan could choose to guide his Jewish thinking, he picked sociology, one of the least factual and most speculative disciplines; it does not speak to the American Jewish skeptic's continuing demand for data.

Kaplan had made sociology his guide because he was anxious to give full play to the heavy post-immigrant emphasis on ethnic-based issues. At the same time, he played down the place of religion in Jewishness, which in his thinking had become an intellectual embarrassment and a social encumbrance. Kaplan's Judaism highlighted Jewish art and literature and other various folkways that made Jews comfortable with one another, and much else that did not involve Jewish faith or law. Today's flowering of klezmer music and Jewish cinema festivals has Kaplan as their long-ago protagonist.

This very breadth of modernized Jewish life led him to advocate turning synagogues into Jewish centers, homes of Jewish folk life in its fullest, in which religion would function as only one of many activities. And yet, this key expression of Kaplan's philosophy has for some time now been almost totally abandoned. While most American Jews may not take their religion very seriously, they have not been willing to make it merely another part of their "folkhood."

Kaplan was far ahead of both the Reform and Conservative movements in his advocacy of Zionism and the revival of Hebrew as our folk tongue. It took some time before the other liberal movements caught up with these enthusiasms. But for all American Jewry's concern with Israeli life, Zionism has not become a central aspect of day-to-day Jewish existence. Our failure to make Hebrew the Yiddish of American Jewish life must pain every lover of *l'shon hakodesh*, our sacred tongue.

Kaplan considered his theology the least significant part of his social theorizing. Nonetheless, with his usual courage he fashioned a way of speaking about God that was breathtakingly daring in the 1930s and still resonates with the religious needs of many people today. Instead of classic Judaism's understanding of people in terms of God, created in the divine image, Kaplan, non–philosophic rationalist that he was, insisted that moderns required a God understood in terms of people's needs. Since we seek fulfillment, what we mean by "God" is everything in nature that helps us fulfill ourselves. In Kaplan's system, God does not command in any way; in Kaplan's methodology, commanding is a function of the mature person and the community.

In one respect I fully agree with Kaplan. On the practical level, most Jews do not care as much about philosophizing as they do about living as a good person and Jew. I would only add that, while Judaism cannot be understood without considering ethnicity seriously, it seems to me that a robust Judaism cannot be created with ethnicity rather than religiosity at its center.

The Greatest Contemporary Orthodox Jewish Philosopher

50

Ever since a 1982 article by David Singer and Moshe Sokol suggested a psychic incoherence in Rabbi Joseph B. Soloveitchik's thought, no one has satisfactorily resolved this issue. Since Rabbi Soloveitchik (hereafter, the Rav, as he was known) was until his death the preeminent halachic and intellectual thinker of "modern" Orthodoxy, the integrity of his thinking deserves a defense.

What powered the Singer-Sokol thesis was the fundamental difference between the Rav's first substantial work, *Ish Hahalakhah* (*Halachic Man*), and his last, lengthy paper, "*Uvikashtem Misham*" (And You Will Seek Me from There [exile]). In theme and method, in tone and concern, they are quite contrary to each other, a perplexity that extends to aspects of his other major writings.

Normally a solution to this issue would be sought by comparing these two essays with the rest of the Rav's work. Unfortunately, even serious students of his thought have not been granted access to the manuscripts he left or to a bibliography informing them what may be made available some day. Until this time, scholars must be most modest when claiming to understand as great a mind as his.

In my own case, there is a further challenge in offering even a tentative resolution: I was not a student of the Rav and therefore cannot state that, in the course of my discipleship, I gained special insight into his thinking that now prompts this proposal. I can only claim to have written the first academic article in English about the Rav's thinking and to have maintained my interest in both understanding and referring to his work over the years. I therefore felt particularly pleased that when we occasionally crossed paths, he was unfailingly cordial to me. This has somehow convinced me that though I was not intellectually close to him, I was an acceptable student of his thought. In this spirit I venture to speculate about what fundamentally unites the major essays he published during his life, despite their considerable diversity.

I believe that the main difficulty in understanding the Rav's thought has been caused by misunderstanding his purpose in writing *Halakhic Man*. I do not mean to propose in any way that the Rav was not fully committed to the classical halachah. Any suggestion like that completely falsifies the Rav's wholehearted dedication to the centrality of the Law in Judaism. Nonetheless, many of his disciples were troubled that non-Orthodox interpretations of Judaism had convinced most American Jews that full-scale halachic observance was not mandated in the modern world. They were thrilled that the Rav had mounted a major defense of the halachah. To his disciples, *Halakhic Man* made an irrefutable case: If a person seriously wanted to call himself or herself a pious Jew, the halachah had to be central to that person's existence. The essay was seen as the Orthodox refutation of the broad appeal of modernist reducers of Jewish obligation—Reform, Conservative, and other minimalizing Jews.

This reading of *Halakhic Man* makes "*Uvikashtem Misham*" quite unsettling, and therefore a deeply disturbing aspect of the Rav's thought. His final article is, in fact, a lengthy, searching, highly personal, and emotionally oriented statement, one that hardly seems the kind of religious confession a halachic man might make. Though it has occasional references to law and obligation, its major concern is the human situation, particularly in times of deep personal anguish. The halachic man continually can look to what the Law requires and what might be driving that obedience; the passionate and suffering believer of the later essay is far more concerned with his feelings and with what his belief leads him to in times of personal distress.

In short, by understanding *Halakhic Man* as a major defense of Orthodoxy, you will have a hard time reconciling "*Uvikashtem Misham.*" I believe that this is probably why, though it is one of the few searching, lengthy statements of the Rav's in print, it remains untranslated nearly thirty years after publication.

I do not consider it presumptuous to suggest that the Rav surely had a sense of the unity behind his works. While he certainly operated on an intellectual level well beyond that of most people, making that integrity known as best we can is an act of faithfulness to his teaching. For myself, this begins with reading *Halakhic Man* somewhat differently than has previously been done. However, that does not minimize its glorification of the halachah. Rather, I wish to call attention in that essay to the standards by which the halachah is elevated. The Rav is at pains to show how extraordinarily rationalistic is a life built on the Law and Jewish legal thinking. That is, making the halachah the grounding axiom of existence requires knowledge of what ruling specifically applies to a given situation. Should there be no exact law covering the case, an analogical rule must be found to yield the relevant law. Should a case arise for which no analogy suggests itself, Halachic Man must exercise his rational creativity in order to determine his duty in this previously unanticipated situation.

In general, when the Law suffuses a person's life, he or she has a rational matrix for responding to the universe in all its wonder. What the Rav is subtly but effectively pointing out in the subtext of this great essay is that one doesn't need to abandon the Law to be that modern ideal, a rationalist. (Note, please, that the specific nature of the rationality demonstrated in the Rav's essay is that of

Hermann Cohen, whose theory of knowledge was the subject of the Rav's University of Berlin doctoral dissertation. Until the Rav's *Halakhic Man*, Cohen's thinking seemed to validate only non-Orthodox Judaism.)

I am suggesting that the Rav had a double purpose in writing *Halakhic Man*. He not only wanted to glorify the life of the Law, he also intended to quietly write a polemic against those who thought they needed to desert traditional Judaism to be fully rational. Years later, when the intellectual climate changed and the passion for rationalism gave way to the intense individualism of existentialism, he did the same thing. The Rav is arguing that a caring Jew does not need to give up the demands and guidance of traditional Judaism in order to face the uncertainties and challenges of human existence. "*Uvikashtem Misham*," while religiously exploring the seismic events of life, also carries on a subtle polemic against existential individualism as a reason for abandoning halachic Judaism and its vision of the inner human life.

The Rav, I am arguing, was a faithful watchman, aware of any new movements that seriously sought to displace traditional Judaism. He was prepared to demonstrate that the new intellectual movements had nothing to offer Jews that Torah had not already anticipated. It also seems to me that this is why the Rav's scope should not be limited to the role of halachic champion but expanded to the more inclusive one of Ish Hatorah, the great expositor and defender of Torah in all its infinite dimensions.

One other consideration persuades me that this analysis has much to commend it. Validating a religious stance by means of a current form of intellectuality—rationalism or existentialism—is originally attractive because it provides a means of bolstering a person's Judaism. However, in due course each subverts personal Jewish faith by demanding to become its authority. What you believe then has to accommodate itself to the outside philosophy, limiting Torah to what your new philosophy will allow. The Rav, I am convinced, understood that intellectual trap and was happy to forgo the benefit of novelty for fear of the ensuing loss it would inevitably bring.

This explains his extraordinary insistence in his essay titled "Confrontation," that we are not only unable to honestly discuss matters of belief with people of other faiths but that *we cannot do so even with people of our own religious community*! I believe the Rav was warning us against the perils of using an intellectual system other than Torah to explain what we believe, lest in translating our innermost beliefs into a commonly available language, we subject them to that language's admissible truth.

Thus the Rav might one day sound like he was justifying Judaism as a higher rationalism and another day as a higher existentialism, or, when it came to interfaith discussion, as a believer in incommunicable religious experience. He was not committed to any modish forms of thinking. For the Rav, the only source of truth was Torah.

The Ethics "Mystery" and Abraham Joshua Heschel

51

I loved the first volume, which appeared in 1999, of the projected two-volume biography of Abraham Joshua Heschel, and not just because one of its two authors, Samuel Dresner, lived two doors down the dormitory hall from me from 1942 to 1944, our first years at Hebrew Union College (HUC). Sam was probably Heschel's most faithful disciple, and when the master left HUC for the Jewish Theological Seminary (JTS) in 1945, Sam went as well. After Heschel died, Sam devoted himself, with a splendid coauthor, Ed Kaplan of Brandeis University, to telling the story of Dr. Heschel's life. (Since Heschel was my teacher too, I feel most comfortable giving him the title by which I always heard him addressed—until recent years, when students, eager to be "more Jewish," began calling him "Rabbi Heschel." Alexander Guttmann, professor of Talmud at the Berlin school where Heschel studied while earning his doctorate at the University of Berlin, and later Heschel's colleague at HUC, gave Heschel his rabbinic ordination, his *s'michah*. Guttmann volunteered the circumstances of that event and I'll gladly pass it on.)

I am prompted to write this by my waning hope that Ed Kaplan might manage to publish the second volume on his own, since Sam died in 2000. In what follows, I want to pay tribute to Heschel as a thinker and not merely as someone whose ethical activism made him known to many American Jews. I want to open up two issues about Heschel's philosophy, as he referred to his views in the subtitles of two early great books: *Man Is Not Alone: A Philosophy of Religion*, and *God in Search of Man: A Philosophy of Judaism*. In the first book mentioned, it would be valuable to have some independent judgment on whether his later efforts to overcome his early praise of time over place in Judaism was reasonably successful. In the second, it would be interesting to know how the absence of a discussion of ethics in his great early masterpieces, as above, became his fervent teaching in his later book, *The Prophets*.

The first problem has to do with the intellectual fallout from his spectacularly successful small book, *The Sabbath: Its Meaning for Modern Man*, which appeared in 1951 and had gone through twenty printings when my 1994 replacement copy appeared. Heschel's fine mind and incomparable style were magnificently synchronized in this work, which glorified Judaism as a religion dedicated to sanctifying time rather than space. Thus the Torah begins with the progression of days of creation and climaxes with the Sabbath, a day devoted to sanctification of self and society rather than to making more things, good as they might be. The book continues by concentrating on what happens in time and foresees its fulfillment in the "end of days." Little as most American Jews in those days knew about their tradition, they knew something about Shabbat and its observances; but they never could have imagined the inner human riches of the day as celebrated here by Heschel.

Despite its extraordinary appeal, *The Sabbath* evoked some sharp criticism. If Judaism was so concerned with time rather than space, why were Jews so determined to return to Palestine, as the land was called prior to 1948, to found their own state there? Was Zionism a sin, as many on the religious right contended? Should those who agreed with Heschel see the Exile from the land and the burdens it placed on Jewish observance as merely another venue for sanctifying time?

Heschel accepted the seriousness of the criticism and added an epilogue to later printings of the book in which, without retracting his characterization of Judaism, he sought to give the Land of Israel special significance in Judaism. The 1967 Six-Day War intensified the issue, particularly because it involved the conquest of Old Jerusalem. Intense pressure was put on the Israelis to give these precious few acres back to Jordan or at least to allow the Old City to be internationalized. Heschel, whose reputation was now at its height, was asked to provide a further defense of this Jewish preoccupation with space. The result was his book, *Israel: An Echo of Eternity*. It is rarely cited by those writing on Heschel. I hope a future biographer will give us a thoughtful evaluation of his efforts to deal with the problem of space in Judaism.

The second matter deals with the likely causes of an unexpected development in Heschel's mature thought. His long-term goal was to reestablish faith in revelation, not in some modernized, person-centered guise, but in a manner that revalidated the commanding power of the classic Jewish tradition. Simply stated, Heschel wanted to restore God's authority in Judaism. This followed decades in which modern Jewish thinkers had promoted different ways for people to usurp Divine authority. Heschel was sophisticated enough to know that this could not be done by mere proclamation but only by an argument grounded in modern terms. He found an acceptable, contemporary style of reasoning in phenomenology; in his doctoral dissertation he analyzed how God's discourse with the prophets, pretty much as the Bible understood it, might have taken place. In those perilous days, one could not earn a doctorate until one's dissertation had been published. In 1936, Heschel finally got the Polish Academy of Sciences to issue his book, *Die Prophetie* (*Prophecy*).

When in 1955 he published his English magnum opus, *God in Search of Man*, Heschel made the same point with a revised strategy. The first of the three sections of the book describes the major ways in which people can experience the reality of God. Heschel argues that if people have really come to know God, they should realize that the Bible gives us the most reliable account of Revelation. Sometime later, the rabbinic tradition carries forward God's demands of us. Although the appeal may be different, Heschel once again asserted the point he made in *Die Prophetie* more than twenty years before.

For American readers, particularly Jews long mesmerized by the picture of Heschel marching with Martin Luther King Jr., it is astonishing that neither book has a significant discussion of ethics. The reason, I believe, is plain enough. Once ethics is introduced into a religious system of thought, its obligations override any supposedly revelatory command that is not clearly ethical, for example, the patriarchal relegation of women to a secondary place in religious life. Since Heschel's goal was to reestablish the Divine foundations of classic Jewish duty, his two basic books make no place for ethics.

However, when in 1962 he issued a revised American version of his dissertation, *The Prophets*, Heschel supplemented his discussion of prophetic consciousness with numerous passionate statements citing their ethical exhortations. Not surprisingly, there is no treatment here (or, I believe, anywhere in his writings) of what we should do if there is a clash between our ethical and our Jewish religious duty. He leaves us with both imperatives making their sometimes-competing claims.

I should like, however, to add some circumstantial evidence about his likely views. In 1982 I was invited by the JTS to participate in a commemoration of Heschel's tenth *yohrtzayt*, the anniversary of his death. After the program, his widow, Sylvia Heschel (who died in 2007) approached to thank me for my remarks. Since I had raised this ethical-halachic issue in the course of my talk, she told me that when their daughter Susie had once said to her father that she was thinking of applying to the seminary as a rabbinical student, she asked if he would endorse her application. He said he would. Some minutes later, Mrs. Heschel approached me again and said something like, "You know, he would have signed Susie's application, but I don't think he would have signed any other woman's."

While I do not expect any future biographer to clarify the clash between ethics and law in Heschel's thinking, it would be interesting to know what prompted him to add the potentially disruptive commitment to ethics to his American book on prophetic consciousness. Was he, already in the late 1950s, involved in and influenced by the civil rights movement? To what extent was this clash residually influenced by his six years at Hebrew Union College, which was, fifteen years earlier, centrally committed to the notion of prophetic Judaism and its essentially ethical view of Jewish duty? Though we are unlikely ever to find a definitive answer, it would certainly be interesting to know what led Heschel to shift his thinking.

Covenant Theology: An Autobiographical Note

52

I'm not sure that I can satisfactorily explain the influence that Protestant Covenant Theology might have had on me in 1961 when I first used the term to characterize an emerging style of Jewish religious thought. I certainly did not know then what this Jewish movement would be like when it received mature treatment thirty years later in my book *Renewing the Covenant*. Back in the post–World War II days, when this thinking first began, several of us shared a few basic views. We believed that God was central to our theology but felt that humanity was also involved with God, working together to produce Judaism's sacred texts and religious traditions. The people of Israel as a whole, not the individual Jew as a single self, served as the historic carrier of an ancient, ongoing relationship with God. Covenant, *brit* in Hebrew, seemed to be the right term to describe this sacred partnership. As the years went by, the term turned out to be a good choice. Nothing I had previously written indicated that I had any knowledge of the right-wing Protestant movement with a similar name. The reconstruction of the period that follows is based on my memory of events taking place about half a century ago. I believe this is a faithful account.

I grew up in Columbus, Ohio, as the child of eastern-European immigrants displaced from New York City. Before I arrived at Ohio

State University in 1940, I had only the most modest sense of what Protestants believed in, a common Jewish experience in those days of quite limited interfaith contacts. For example, my Boy Scout troop met in the basement of a Protestant church, yet I have no idea, even now, what denomination it was. There was certainly no teaching about religion in my senior high school.

Ohio State University had no department of religion. Since I was happy as a Jew, I was not at all concerned by its lack. What I acquired there was secular philosophy and the psychology of personality. So when I came to the Hebrew Union College (HUC) in 1942 (I graduated in 1948), I discovered how little I knew from several schoolmates with a more sophisticated education than my own. I did learn, however, that almost none of my rabbinical-school colleagues were interested in theology.

It took me some time to find Arnold Jacob Wolf, a fifth generation American brought up in Chicago's classic Reform Judaism, and Steven S. Schwarzschild, a child of Frankfurt and Berlin, most recently of New York. Both were fellow 1948 HUC ordainees, and like me, both were interested in serious thinking about Jewish belief—but they also knew how to start doing it. They both had a decent background in Protestant thought, though neither they nor any of the publications they introduced me to said anything about Protestant Covenant Theology. We did make one in-depth effort to see if Christian thinking could indicate how we might get beyond Jewish rationalism's focus on universalism and its limited sense of God; we read Reinhold Niebuhr's Gifford Lectures, *The Nature and Destiny of Man*, but that too said nothing of Covenant Theology.

In some of our HUC classes, the professors gave us a modest sense of what concerned Protestant academics, focusing mainly on the nineteenth and early twentieth-century German intellectual giants—no Covenant Theologians among them. I recall no significant reference to contemporary thinkers. This was partially remedied by an annual exchange lectureship between HUC and leading

Christian seminaries, so we did get to hear from some important Protestant leaders. Only once did an actual theologian address us, Reinhold Niebuhr no less, who talked about the dialectic of the self and not about Covenant.

What is more directly relevant to this topic is how, as my schooling progressed, I developed an agenda of my own. Briefly put, I knew I was a modern and I didn't need much reinforcement on that score. But I increasingly began puzzling over what it meant for someone like me to be a Jew. That concern for the Jewish side of my being led me to a basic methodological problem: If, as was the common intellectual practice, Jews like me showed our modernity by adopting the procedures of acclaimed Christian thinkers, weren't we allowing *them* to tell *us* what Judaism needed to be today? Thus if we took the rational route and let the great nineteenth-century philosophers of religion (all German Protestants) guide us, weren't we for all intents and purposes letting Immanuel Kant or Georg Wilhelm Friedrich Hegel define our Judaism?

The double bind here, of course, is that if we wanted to speak of our Judaism in terms of its modern evolution, we would have to explain ourselves in a Protestant-influenced intellectual manner. In various forms, that problem of speaking our inner truth in an alien tongue plagued me for decades. I mention it here because it indicates the critical mindset with which I approached the task of educating myself in contemporary religious thought.

In my view, a few facts about my maturing work bolster my memory of an increasing effort to do Jewish theology as much from the inside out as from the outside in. So, in defiance of the common view that the best doorway into Jewish religious thought was the study of medieval Jewish philosophy, I was determined to ground myself in rabbinic thought. I did my rabbinic thesis in1948, long before electronic retrieval eased things, on "The Rabbinic Doctrine of Torah" and my Doctor of Hebrew Letters dissertation in 1952 on "Universalism and Particularism in the Tannaitic Midrashim." (In nonacademic jargon, this means the positive and negative views of gentiles as found in some of the earliest rabbinic books.)

When in 1956 I entered the Columbia University–Union Theological Seminary joint program in the philosophy of religion, I studied with Reinhold Niebuhr, the most eminent mid-twentieth-century American theologian; his associate, John Bennet; John Baillee, a Scottish theologian of international repute; and various other professors. To the best of my knowledge, none of them ever mentioned Protestant Covenant Theology. I was "ABD" (all but dissertation) when I applied this work to an education doctoral program. I wrote my dissertation for that degree in 1958 by showing how the concept of the Covenant might be used to structure a volume explaining Jewish belief to Jewish educators. I was committed to the idea of explaining contemporary Judaism as much from an inside point of view as from what modern thought might make of it.

As I remember, I subsequently came across the notion of Protestant Covenant Theology in some of my reading. It struck me as surprisingly irrelevant to what the Jewish notion of covenantalism entailed, namely, God's relationship with the Jewish people, individually and collectively, and the obligations that flowed from it. So when I was searching for a term that characterized the groping of the few of us who were devoted to the task of producing a new Jewish theology, "Covenant," with its relational involvement of God, the Jewish people, and Jewish duty, quickly suggested itself.

In the near half century since I chose the term, I do not recall having any second thoughts about its aptness.

GLOSSARY

Adon Olam: "Lord of the universe"; a title of God; also a Hebrew hymn praising God.

Adonai: "My Lord," a title of God generally used as a euphemism for God's unpronounced four-letter name. *See* "Tetragrammaton."

Adonai echad: "*Adonai* is One"; the religiously critical conclusion of the Shema.

aggadah: "Lore"; in rabbinic literature, all material that is not law; recommended but not binding.

agunah: "Chained one"; more commonly, the term for a woman whose husband will not grant her a religiously valid divorce.

ahavat Yisrael: "Love of Israel," that is, the Jewish people; a major Jewish virtue.

Aleinu: "It is incumbent on us" (to praise God); the first word and thus the title of the first concluding prayer of Jewish worship services.

Amidah: "Standing" [prayer]; the title for the block of prayers that is the center of every Jewish service.

atzilah: "Emanation"; the highest of the four kabbalistic dimensions of reality, the others in descending order being: *beriyah*, creation; *yetzirah*, forming; and *asiyah*, making.

aveilei tziyon: "Mourners of Zion"; originally a term for mystics who bewailed the destruction of Jerusalem.

Avinu Malkeinu: "Our Father, our King"; best known as the first words of a major prayer for forgiveness said during High Holy Day services; also used elsewhere in Jewish worship.

Baruch: "Blessed, praised"; the opening word of the many Jewish blessings to God, whether acknowledging God's daily involvement with us or said in Jewish worship.

bet din: Jewish court.

Borei Olam: "Creator of the Universe"; a name for God.

B'rachot: "Blessings": title of the first tractate of the Talmud.

d'var Torah: "A word of Torah" (instruction); now used for less formal Jewish speaking.

daven: Term, probably of Arabic origin, whose meaning has come to mean "to pray."

Elul: Hebrew calendar month that comes immediately before Rosh Hashanah.

En Sof: "Without End"; the kabbalistic term for God as God is in God-self, about which all speech is inadequate.

genevat da'at: "Giving a false impression."

HaGevurah: "The Power"; rabbinic name for God.

HaKadosh Baruch Hu: "The Holy One, blessed be He"; common rabbinic name for God.

halachah (pl. **halachot**): "Walking"; in rabbinic literature, Law.

halachah lemaaseh: Legal pronouncement of practical not theoretical effect.

HaMakom: "The Place"; rabbinic name for God.

Hasid: A Jewish pietist; an adherent of Hasidism.

Hatzi Kaddish: "Half *Kaddish*"; prayer that separates sections of worship service.

havurah (pl. **havurot**): Informal group emphasizing interpersonal relationships.

herem: Term for the fullest level of Jewish community ostracism and thus the Jewish equivalent of excommunication.

hesed: Loving-kindness, benevolence; a major quality of God and a prime Jewish virtue.

Ish Hatorah: "Man of the Torah"; used here to describe an ideal Jew.

Kabbalah: Literally, "reception" and thus its early use to mean "tradition"; now more commonly used to describe Jewish mystical teaching.

Kabbalat Shabbat: Welcoming the Sabbath with prayer and ceremony.

Kaddish: Aramaic prayer praising God, used in various forms in services and other moments in Jewish life, most commonly known for its recitation by mourners.

Kaddish Yatom: The special form of the Kaddish recited by mourners.

Karaites: Persian Jewish sect from ca. 700 CE who rejected the Oral Torah and accepted only the Bible as sacred.

kavanah: "Intention," the ideal for all Jewish religious acts but halachically required only in special situations, like reciting the Sh'ma.

kavod: "Honor," a term used of God and human beings, calling attention to the special sense of "weightiness" one feels in the presence of the great or mighty.

ketubah (pl. *k'tubot*): Jewish marriage contract. *See K'tubot.*

Kiddush: "Sanctifying," used for the blessing over the wine on festive Jewish occasions.

K'tubot: Name of tractate in the Talmudic order of "Women."

mameloshen: "Mother tongue"; commonly used to refer to Yiddish.

mellah: North African term for areas of Jewish settlement; roughly equivalent to eastern-European shtetl or western-European ghetto.

mensch: German for man or person, often used to transliterate the Yiddish equivalent.

mentsh: The transliteration used here for the Yiddish word for man or person.

midrash: Interpretation of a biblical text, often quite imaginative.

minhag (pl. *minhagim*): Custom(s).

Mishneh Torah: "The Torah Restated"; a phrase used for the Book of Deuteronomy; also used by Maimonides in the late twelfth century as a title for his pathbreaking code of Jewish law.

mitzvah (pl. *mitzvot*): Commandment, good deed.

nechemta: "Consolation"; commonly used to describe the conclusion of any speech that, by folk tradition, should be consoling and is often messianic.

N'ilah: "Locking up"; the Yom Kippur final service whose symbolism derives from the Temple practice of closing the gates at sunset.

Noahides: The children of Noah; all humankind.

Oneg Shabbat: "Sabbath joy"; refers to celebrations in connection with the Sabbath.

posek: One who is recognized as an authoritative halachic decision maker.

prosbul: Legal device by which Hillel (first century BCE) made it possible for those who wished to make loans as the Sabbatical year approached (when all Jewish loans were to be forgiven) by assigning them to the court and thus protecting the lender's capital.

rav: Shortened form of "rabbi"; "The Rav" is used in the modern Orthodox community to refer to the late teacher Rabbi Joseph B. Soloveitchik.

rebbe: A Yiddishization of the Hebrew "rav" or "rabi"; commonly used to refer to leaders of Hasidic groups.

R'faenu: Prayer in the daily service in which one prays for the recovery from illness of one's relatives and friends as well as for all who are sick.

r'fuah shelemah: "Complete healing" for which one prays for the sick.

r'tzono: "His [God's] will"; Hebrew for the Aramaic *r'uteih* in the Kaddish prayer, which speaks of God's will in creating the universe.

seder: Order; the Passover pre- and post-dinner celebration of the Exodus from Egypt.

Sefer Hasidim: "The Book of the Pious"; a late twelfth-century compilation of the teachings and practices of German Jewish pietists, known for their ethics and self-mortification.

Sefer T'hillim: The Book of Psalms.

s'firot: "Spheres"; almost exclusively used to refer to the ten nodes of God's power and functioning, a unique and essential part of kabbalistic theory.

Shabbat: "The Sabbath"; in the Ashkenazic pronunciation it is *Shabbos.*

Shacharit: The Jewish morning service.

Shavuot: "Weeks"; the festival that comes seven weeks and a day after Passover and commemorates the giving of the Torah.

Shechinah: A Rabbinic term for God's Indwelling Presence, generally understood as feminine.

Shema: "Hear" almost always refers to the statement of God's unity; the heart of Jewish religious belief.

shivah: "Seven"; expression used for the intense period of mourning after the death of a close relative.

sh'mei rabbah: "The Great Name"; Aramaic phrase from the Kaddish prayer used as a euphemism for God's greatness.

shtetl: A small village of eastern Europe with a large Jewish population.

shtieblach: Yiddish for small buildings that functioned like American storefront shuls.

shul: Yiddish for "synagogue."

sh'virah: "Smashing up"; the second of the three stages of the Lurianic mystic teaching about creation. *See tzimtzum.*

Simchat Torah: "The Rejoicing of the Torah"; the final day of Sukkot, on which the cycle of Torah reading is completed and begun anew.

s'michah: "The laying of hands" to grant authority; rabbinical ordination.

Sukkot: The fall harvest Festival of Booths (singular, sukkah) that begins five days after Yom Kippur and lasts for nine days, during which Jews symbolically live in booths in commemoration of the Exodus from Egypt.

talmid hacham: A sage.

talmud Torah: Study of sacred texts.

Tetragrammaton: The four-consonant personal name of God, articulated only once a year by the High Priest emerging from the Temple's Holy of Holies on Yom Kippur, and never since the destruction of the Second Temple in 70 CE.

tikkun: "Restoration"; in the Lurianic mystic system of creation, the third step. *See tzimtzum.*

t'reif: Not kosher and thus forbidden.

t'shuvot: "Responses"; answers to questions of Jewish law, the halachic equivalent of case law.

tzaddik: "Righteous person"; also refers to the leader of a Hasidic sect.

tzedakah: "Righteousness"; often used to refer to the specific duty of giving charity.

tzimtzum: "Contraction"; in the Lurianic mystic system, the first of three phases of creation, followed by *sh'virah*, smashing up of the vessels expected to contain the creation. Jewish life then is devoted to *tikkun*, mystically restoring the sparks still latent in created things so that the world will finally be whole.

yeshiva bocher: Young (male) scholar attending a religious academy.

Yigdal: Hebrew hymn whose lyrics present a condensed version of the thirteen principles that Maimonides said every Jew should affirm.

yohrtzayt: "Year's time"; Yiddish for the anniversary of the death of a close relative, when special rituals are performed.

Bibliography of Titles Mentioned in This Book

Baeck, Leo. *The Essence of Judaism*. New York: Macmillan, 1936.

Borowitz, Eugene B. *Liberal Judaism*. New York: UAHC Press, 1984.

———. *Renewing the Covenant: A Theology for the Postmodern Jew*. Philadelphia: The Jewish Publication Society, 1991.

Buber, Martin. *I and Thou*. Edinburgh: T. and T. Clark, 1937.

Cohen, Hermann. *Religion of Reason out of the Sources of Judaism*. New York: Frederick Ungar, 1972.

Herberg, Will. *Judaism and Modern Man*. New York: Farrar, Straus and Young, 1951.

Heschel, Abraham J. *Die Prophetie*. Krakow: Nakladem Polskiej Akademji Umiejetnosci, 1936.

———. *God in Search of Man*. Philadelphia: Jewish Publication Society, 1956.

———. *Israel: An Echo of Eternity*. Woodstock, VT: Jewish Lights, 1997.

———. *The Prophets*. Philadelphia: Jewish Publication Society, 1962.

———. *The Sabbath: Its Meaning for Modern Man*. New York: Farrar, Straus and Giroux, 1951.

Kaplan, Mordecai. *Judaism as a Civilization*. New York: Macmillan, 1934.

Kohler, Kaufmann. *Jewish Theology, Systematically and Historically Considered*. New York: Macmillan, 1918.

Mackler, Aaron. "Cases and Principles in Jewish Bioethics: Toward a Holistic Model," in Eliot Dorff and Louis Newman. *Contemporary Jewish Ethics and Morality*. New York: Oxford, 1995.

Niebuhr, Reinhold, *The Nature and Destiny of Man*. 2 vols. New York: Scribners, 1941–43.

Plaskow, Judith. *Standing Again at Sinai*. San Francisco: Harper & Row, 1990.

Soloveitchik, Joseph B. *Halachic Man*. Philadelphia: Jewish Publication Society, 1983.

Steinberg, Milton. *As a Driven Leaf*. Indianapolis: Bobbs-Merrill, 1934.

———. *Basic Judaism*. New York: Harcourt, Brace, 1947.

Bar/Bat Mitzvah

The JGirl's Guide: The Young Jewish Woman's Handbook for Coming of Age
By Penina Adelman, Ali Feldman, and Shulamit Reinharz This inspirational, interactive guidebook helps pre-teen Jewish girls address the many issues surrounding coming of age. 6 x 9, 240 pp, Quality PB, 978-1-58023-215-9 **$14.99** *For ages 11 & up*
Also Available: **The JGirl's Teacher's and Parent's Guide**
8½ x 11, 56 pp, PB, 978-1-58023-225-8 **$8.99**

Bar/Bat Mitzvah Basics, 2nd Edition: A Practical Family Guide to Coming of Age Together *Edited by Cantor Helen Leneman* 6 x 9, 240 pp, Quality PB, 978-1-58023-151-0 **$18.95**

The Bar/Bat Mitzvah Memory Book, 2nd Edition: An Album for Treasuring the Spiritual Celebration *By Rabbi Jeffrey K. Salkin and Nina Salkin*
8 x 10, 48 pp, 2-color text, Deluxe HC, ribbon marker, 978-1-58023-263-0 **$19.99**

For Kids—Putting God on Your Guest List, 2nd Edition: How to Claim the Spiritual Meaning of Your Bar or Bat Mitzvah *By Rabbi Jeffrey K. Salkin*
6 x 9, 144 pp, Quality PB, 978-1-58023-308-8 **$15.99** *For ages 11–13*

Putting God on the Guest List, 3rd Edition: How to Reclaim the Spiritual Meaning of Your Child's Bar or Bat Mitzvah *By Rabbi Jeffrey K. Salkin*
6 x 9, 224 pp, Quality PB, 978-1-58023-222-7 **$16.99**; HC, 978-1-58023-260-9 **$24.99**
Also Available: **Putting God on the Guest List Teacher's Guide**
8½ x 11, 48 pp, PB, 978-1-58023-226-5 **$8.99**

Tough Questions Jews Ask: A Young Adult's Guide to Building a Jewish Life
By Rabbi Edward Feinstein 6 x 9, 160 pp, Quality PB, 978-1-58023-139-8 **$14.99** *For ages 11 & up*
Also Available: **Tough Questions Jews Ask Teacher's Guide**
8½ x 11, 72 pp, PB, 978-1-58023-187-9 **$8.95**

Bible Study/Midrash

The Modern Men's Torah Commentary: New Insights from Jewish Men on the 54 Weekly Torah Portions *Edited by Rabbi Jeffrey K. Salkin*
A major contribution to modern biblical commentary. Addresses the most important concerns of modern men by opening them up to the life of Torah.
6 x 9, 368 pp, HC, 978-1-58023-395-8 **$24.99**

The Genesis of Leadership: What the Bible Teaches Us about Vision, Values and Leading Change *By Rabbi Nathan Laufer; Foreword by Senator Joseph I. Lieberman*
Unlike other books on leadership, this one is rooted in the stories of the Bible.
6 x 9, 288 pp, Quality PB, 978-1-58023-352-1 **$18.99**

Hineini in Our Lives: Learning How to Respond to Others through 14 Biblical Texts and Personal Stories *By Rabbi Norman J. Cohen, PhD* 6 x 9, 240 pp, Quality PB, 978-1-58023-274-6 **$16.99**

Moses and the Journey to Leadership: Timeless Lessons of Effective Management from the Bible and Today's Leaders *By Rabbi Norman J. Cohen, PhD*
6 x 9, 240 pp, Quality PB, 978-1-58023-351-4 **$18.99**; HC, 978-1-58023-227-2 **$21.99**

Self, Struggle & Change: Family Conflict Stories in Genesis and Their Healing Insights for Our Lives *By Rabbi Norman J. Cohen, PhD* 6 x 9, 224 pp, Quality PB, 978-1-879045-66-8 **$18.99**

The Triumph of Eve & Other Subversive Bible Tales *By Matt Biers-Ariel*
5½ x 8½, 192 pp, Quality PB, 978-1-59473-176-1 **$14.99**
(A book from SkyLight Paths, Jewish Lights' sister imprint)

The Wisdom of Judaism: An Introduction to the Values of the Talmud
By Rabbi Dov Peretz Elkins Explores the essence of Judaism through reflections on the words of the rabbinic sages. 6 x 9, 192 pp, Quality PB, 978-1-58023-327-9 **$16.99**
Also Available: **The Wisdom of Judaism Teacher's Guide**
8½ x 11, 18 pp, PB, 978-1-58023-350-7 **$8.99**

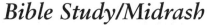

Or phone, fax, mail or e-mail to: **JEWISH LIGHTS** Publishing
Sunset Farm Offices, Route 4 • P.O. Box 237 • Woodstock, Vermont 05091
Tel: (802) 457-4000 • Fax: (802) 457-4004 • www.jewishlights.com
Credit card orders: **(800) 962-4544** (8:30AM–5:30PM ET Monday–Friday)
Generous discounts on quantity orders. SATISFACTION GUARANTEED. Prices subject to change.

Congregation Resources

Building a Successful Volunteer Culture
Finding Meaning in Service in the Jewish Community
By Rabbi Charles Simon; Foreword by Shelley Lindauer; Preface by Dr. Ron Wolfson
Shows you how to develop and maintain the volunteers who are essential to the vitality of your organization and community. 6 x 9, 192 pp, Quality PB, 978-1-58023-408-5 **$16.99**

The Case for Jewish Peoplehood: Can We Be One?
By Dr. Erica Brown and Dr. Misha Galperin; Foreword by Rabbi Joseph Telushkin
Explores the purpose, possibilities and limitations of peoplehood as a unifying concept of community for a people struggling profoundly with Jewish identity.
6 x 9, 224 pp, HC, 978-1-58023-401-6 **$21.99**

Finding a Spiritual Home: How a New Generation of Jews Can Transform the American
Synagogue *By Rabbi Sidney Schwarz* 6 x 9, 352 pp, Quality PB, 978-1-58023-185-5 **$19.95**

Inspired Jewish Leadership: Practical Approaches to Building Strong Communities
By Dr. Erica Brown 6 x 9, 256 pp, HC, 978-1-58023-361-3 **$24.99**

Jewish Pastoral Care, 2nd Edition: A Practical Handbook from Traditional &
Contemporary Sources *Edited by Rabbi Dayle A. Friedman, MSW, MAJCS, BCC*
6 x 9, 528 pp, HC, 978-1-58023-221-0 **$40.00**

Jewish Spiritual Direction: An Innovative Guide from Traditional and
Contemporary Sources *Edited by Rabbi Howard A. Addison and Barbara Eve Breitman, MSW*
6 x 9, 368 pp, HC, 978-1-58023-230-2 **$30.00**

Rethinking Synagogues: A New Vocabulary for Congregational Life
By Rabbi Lawrence A. Hoffman 6 x 9, 240 pp, Quality PB, 978-1-58023-248-7 **$19.99**

Spiritual Community: The Power to Restore Hope, Commitment and Joy
By Rabbi David A. Teutsch, PhD 5½ x 8½, 144 pp, HC, 978-1-58023-270-8 **$19.99**

The Spirituality of Welcoming: How to Transform Your Congregation into a
Sacred Community *By Dr. Ron Wolfson* 6 x 9, 224 pp, Quality PB, 978-1-58023-244-9 **$19.99**

Children's Books

What You Will See Inside a Synagogue
By Rabbi Lawrence A. Hoffman, PhD, and Dr. Ron Wolfson; Full-color photos by Bill Aron
A colorful, fun-to-read introduction that explains the ways and whys of Jewish worship and religious life. 8½ x 10½, 32 pp, Full-color photos, Quality PB, 978-1-59473-256-0 **$8.99**
For ages 6 & up (A book from SkyLight Paths, Jewish Lights' sister imprint)

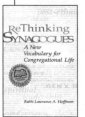

Because Nothing Looks Like God
By Lawrence Kushner and Karen Kushner Introduces children to the possibilities of spiritual life. 11 x 8½, 32 pp, Full-color illus., HC, 978-1-58023-092-6 **$17.99** *For ages 4 & up*
Board Book Companions to *Because Nothing Looks Like God*
5 x 5, 24 pp, Full-color illus., SkyLight Paths Board Books *For ages 0–4*
What Does God Look Like? 978-1-893361-23-2 **$7.99**
How Does God Make Things Happen? 978-1-893361-24-9 **$7.95**
Where Is God? 978-1-893361-17-1 **$7.99**

The Book of Miracles: A Young Person's Guide to Jewish Spiritual Awareness
Written and illus. by Lawrence Kushner
6 x 9, 96 pp, 2-color illus., HC, 978-1-879045-78-1 **$16.95** *For ages 9 & up*

In God's Hands
By Lawrence Kushner and Gary Schmidt 9 x 12, 32 pp, HC, 978-1-58023-224-1 **$16.99**

In Our Image: God's First Creatures *By Nancy Sohn Swartz*
9 x 12, 32 pp, Full-color illus., HC, 978-1-879045-99-6 **$16.95** *For ages 4 & up*
Also Available as a Board Book: **How Did the Animals Help God?**
5 x 5, 24 pp, Full-color illus., Board Book, 978-1-59473-044-3 **$7.99** *For ages 0–4*
(A book from SkyLight Paths, Jewish Lights' sister imprint)

The Kids' Fun Book of Jewish Time
By Emily Sper 9 x 7½, 24 pp, Full-color illus., HC, 978-1-58023-311-8 **$16.99**

What Makes Someone a Jew? *By Lauren Seidman*
Reflects the changing face of American Judaism.
10 x 8½, 32 pp, Full-color photos, Quality PB, 978-1-58023-321-7 **$8.99** *For ages 3–6*

Children's Books by Sandy Eisenberg Sasso

Adam & Eve's First Sunset: God's New Day
Engaging new story explores fear and hope, faith and gratitude in ways that will delight kids and adults—inspiring us to bless each of God's days and nights.
9 x 12, 32 pp, Full-color illus., HC, 978-1-58023-177-0 **$17.95** *For ages 4 & up*

Also Available as a Board Book: **Adam and Eve's New Day**
5 x 5, 24 pp, Full-color illus., Board Book, 978-1-59473-205-8 **$7.99** *For ages 0–4*
(A book from SkyLight Paths, Jewish Lights' sister imprint)

But God Remembered: Stories of Women from Creation to the Promised Land   Four different stories of women—Lilith, Serach, Bityah and the Daughters of Z—teach us important values through their faith and actions.
9 x 12, 32 pp, Full-color illus., Quality PB, 978-1-58023-372-9 **$8.99** *For ages 8 & up*

Cain & Abel: Finding the Fruits of Peace
Shows children that we have the power to deal with anger in positive ways. Provides questions for kids and adults to explore together.
9 x 12, 32 pp, Full-color illus., HC, 978-1-58023-123-7 **$16.95** *For ages 5 & up*

God in Between
If you wanted to find God, where would you look? This magical, mythical tale teaches that God can be found where we are: within all of us and the relationships between us.   9 x 12, 32 pp, Full-color illus., HC, 978-1-879045-86-6 **$16.95** *For ages 4 & up*

God's Paintbrush: Special 10th Anniversary Edition
Wonderfully interactive, invites children of all faiths and backgrounds to encounter God through moments in their own lives. Provides questions adult and child can explore together.   11 x 8½, 32 pp, Full-color illus., HC, 978-1-58023-195-4 **$17.95** *For ages 4 & up*

Also Available as a Board Book: **I Am God's Paintbrush**
5 x 5, 24 pp, Full-color illus., Board Book, 978-1-59473-265-2 **$7.99** *For ages 0–4*
(A book from SkyLight Paths, Jewish Lights' sister imprint)

Also Available: **God's Paintbrush Teacher's Guide**
8½ x 11, 32 pp, PB, 978-1-879045-57-6 **$8.95**

God's Paintbrush Celebration Kit
A Spiritual Activity Kit for Teachers and Students of All Faiths, All Backgrounds
9½ x 12, 40 Full-color Activity Sheets & Teacher Folder w/ complete instructions
HC, 978-1-58023-050-6 **$21.95**
8-Student Activity Sheet Pack (40 sheets/5 sessions), 978-1-58023-058-2 **$19.95**

In God's Name
Like an ancient myth in its poetic text and vibrant illustrations, this award-winning modern fable about the search for God's name celebrates the diversity and, at the same time, the unity of all people.
9 x 12, 32 pp, Full-color illus., HC, 978-1-879045-26-2 **$16.99** *For ages 4 & up*

Also Available as a Board Book: **What Is God's Name?**
5 x 5, 24 pp, Full-color illus., Board Book, 978-1-893361-10-2 **$7.99** *For ages 0–4*
(A book from SkyLight Paths, Jewish Lights' sister imprint)

Also Available in Spanish: **El nombre de Dios**
9 x 12, 32 pp, Full-color illus., HC, 978-1-893361-63-8 **$16.95**

Noah's Wife: The Story of Naamah
When God tells Noah to bring the animals of the world onto the ark, God also calls on Naamah, Noah's wife, to save each plant on Earth. Based on an ancient text.
9 x 12, 32 pp, Full-color illus., HC, 978-1-58023-134-3 **$16.95** *For ages 4 & up*

Also Available as a Board Book: **Naamah, Noah's Wife**
5 x 5, 24 pp, Full-color illus., Board Book, 978-1-893361-56-0 **$7.95** For ages 0–4
(A book from SkyLight Paths, Jewish Lights' sister imprint)

For Heaven's Sake
Heaven is often found where you least expect it.
9 x 12, 32 pp, Full-color illus., HC, 978-1-58023-054-4 **$16.95** *For ages 4 & up*

God Said Amen
An inspiring story about hearing the answers to our prayers.
9 x 12, 32 pp, Full-color illus., HC, 978-1-58023-080-3 **$16.95** *For ages 4 & up*

Meditation

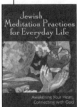

Jewish Meditation Practices for Everyday Life
Awakening Your Heart, Connecting with God
By Rabbi Jeff Roth
Offers a fresh take on meditation that draws on life experience and living life with greater clarity as opposed to the traditional method of rigorous study.
6 x 9, 224 pp, Quality PB Original, 978-1-58023-397-2 **$18.99**

The Handbook of Jewish Meditation Practices
A Guide for Enriching the Sabbath and Other Days of Your Life
By Rabbi David A. Cooper Easy-to-learn meditation techniques.
6 x 9, 208 pp, Quality PB, 978-1-58023-102-2 **$16.95**

Discovering Jewish Meditation: Instruction & Guidance for Learning an Ancient
Spiritual Practice *By Nan Fink Gefen, PhD* 6 x 9, 208 pp, Quality PB, 978-1-58023-067-4 **$16.95**

Meditation from the Heart of Judaism: Today's Teachers Share Their Practices,
Techniques, and Faith *Edited by Avram Davis*
6 x 9, 256 pp, Quality PB, 978-1-58023-049-0 **$16.95**

Ritual/Sacred Practices

The Jewish Dream Book: The Key to Opening the Inner Meaning of
Your Dreams *By Vanessa L. Ochs, PhD, with Elizabeth Ochs; Illus. by Kristina Swarner*
Instructions for how modern people can perform ancient Jewish dream practices and dream interpretations drawn from the Jewish wisdom tradition.
8 x 8, 128 pp, Full-color illus., Deluxe PB w/ flaps, 978-1-58023-132-9 **$16.95**

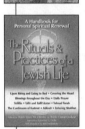

God in Your Body: Kabbalah, Mindfulness and Embodied Spiritual Practice
By Jay Michaelson
The first comprehensive treatment of the body in Jewish spiritual practice and an essential guide to the sacred.
6 x 9, 272 pp, Quality PB, 978-1-58023-304-0 **$18.99**

The Book of Jewish Sacred Practices: CLAL's Guide to Everyday & Holiday
Rituals & Blessings *Edited by Rabbi Irwin Kula and Vanessa L. Ochs, PhD*
6 x 9, 368 pp, Quality PB, 978-1-58023-152-7 **$18.95**

Jewish Ritual: A Brief Introduction for Christians
By Rabbi Kerry M. Olitzky and Rabbi Daniel Judson
5½ x 8½, 144 pp, Quality PB, 978-1-58023-210-4 **$14.99**

The Rituals & Practices of a Jewish Life: A Handbook for Personal Spiritual
Renewal *Edited by Rabbi Kerry M. Olitzky and Rabbi Daniel Judson*
6 x 9, 272 pp, illus., Quality PB, 978-1-58023-169-5 **$18.95**

The Sacred Art of Lovingkindness: Preparing to Practice
By Rabbi Rami Shapiro 5½ x 8½, 176 pp, Quality PB, 978-1-59473-151-8 **$16.99**
(A book from SkyLight Paths, Jewish Lights' sister imprint)

Science Fiction/Mystery & Detective Fiction

Criminal Kabbalah: An Intriguing Anthology of Jewish Mystery &
Detective Fiction *Edited by Lawrence W. Raphael; Foreword by Laurie R. King*
All-new stories from twelve of today's masters of mystery and detective fiction—sure to delight mystery buffs of all faith traditions.
6 x 9, 256 pp, Quality PB, 978-1-58023-109-1 **$16.95**

Mystery Midrash: An Anthology of Jewish Mystery & Detective Fiction
Edited by Lawrence W. Raphael; Preface by Joel Siegel
6 x 9, 304 pp, Quality PB, 978-1-58023-055-1 **$16.95**

Wandering Stars: An Anthology of Jewish Fantasy & Science Fiction
Edited by Jack Dann; Introduction by Isaac Asimov
6 x 9, 272 pp, Quality PB, 978-1-58023-005-6 **$18.99**

More Wandering Stars: An Anthology of Outstanding Stories of Jewish Fantasy and
Science Fiction *Edited by Jack Dann; Introduction by Isaac Asimov*
6 x 9, 192 pp, Quality PB, 978-1-58023-063-6 **$16.95**

Spirituality/Women's Interest

The Divine Feminine in Biblical Wisdom Literature: Selections Annotated & Explained *Translated & Annotated by Rabbi Rami Shapiro* 5½ x 8½, 240 pp, Quality PB, 978-1-59473-109-9 **$16.99** *(A book from SkyLight Paths, Jewish Lights' sister imprint)*

The Quotable Jewish Woman: Wisdom, Inspiration & Humor from the Mind & Heart *Edited by Elaine Bernstein Partnow* 6 x 9, 496 pp, Quality PB, 978-1-58023-236-4 **$19.99**

The Women's Haftarah Commentary: New Insights from Women Rabbis on the 54 Weekly Haftarah Portions, the 5 Megillot & Special Shabbatot *Edited by Rabbi Elyse Goldstein* 6 x 9, 560 pp, Quality PB, 978-1-58023-371-2 **$19.99**

The Women's Torah Commentary: New Insights from Women Rabbis on the 54 Weekly Torah Portions *Edited by Rabbi Elyse Goldstein* 6 x 9, 496 pp, Quality PB, 978-1-58023-370-5 **$19.99**; HC, 978-1-58023-076-6 **$34.95**

The Year Mom Got Religion: One Woman's Midlife Journey into Judaism *By Lee Meyerhoff Hendler* 6 x 9, 208 pp, Quality PB, 978-1-58023-070-4 **$15.95**

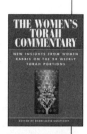

Spirituality/Crafts
(from SkyLight Paths, Jewish Lights' sister imprint)

Beading—The Creative Spirit: Finding Your Sacred Center through the Art of Beadwork *By Wendy Ellsworth*
Invites you on a spiritual pilgrimage into the kaleidoscope world of glass and color.
7 x 9, 240 pp, 8-page full-color insert, b/w photos and diagrams, Quality PB, 978-1-59473-267-6 **$18.99**

Contemplative Crochet: A Hands-On Guide for Interlocking Faith and Craft *By Cindy Crandall-Frazier; Foreword by Linda Skolnik*
Will take you on a path deeper into your crocheting and your spiritual awareness.
7 x 9, 208 pp, b/w photos, Quality PB, 978-1-59473-238-6 **$16.99**

The Knitting Way: A Guide to Spiritual Self-Discovery *By Linda Skolnik and Janice MacDaniels* Shows how to use the practice of knitting to strengthen our spiritual selves. 7 x 9, 240 pp, b/w photos, Quality PB, 978-1-59473-079-5 **$16.99**

The Quilting Path: A Guide to Spiritual Self-Discovery through Fabric, Thread and Kabbalah *By Louise Silk* Explores how to cultivate personal growth through quilt making. 7 x 9, 192 pp, b/w photos, Quality PB, 978-1-59473-206-5 **$16.99**

The Painting Path: Embodying Spiritual Discovery through Yoga, Brush and Color *By Linda Novick; Foreword by Richard Segalman*
Explores the divine connection you can experience through art.
7 x 9, 208 pp, 8-page full-color insert, b/w photos, Quality PB, 978-1-59473-226-3 **$18.99**

The Scrapbooking Journey: A Hands-On Guide to Spiritual Discovery *By Cory Richardson-Lauve; Foreword by Stacy Julian*
Reveals how this craft can become a practice used to deepen and shape your life.
7 x 9, 176 pp, 8-page full-color insert, b/w photos, Quality PB, 978-1-59473-216-4 **$18.99**

Travel

Israel—A Spiritual Travel Guide, 2nd Edition A Companion for the Modern Jewish Pilgrim *By Rabbi Lawrence A. Hoffman, PhD* 4¾ x 10, 256 pp, illus., Quality PB, 978-1-58023-261-6 **$18.99**

Also Available: **The Israel Mission Leader's Guide** 5½ x 8½, 16 pp, PB, 978-1-58023-085-8 **$4.95**

12-Step

100 Blessings Every Day: Daily Twelve Step Recovery Affirmations, Exercises for Personal Growth & Renewal Reflecting Seasons of the Jewish Year *By Rabbi Kerry M. Olitzky; Foreword by Rabbi Neil Gillman, PhD* 4½ x 6¼, 432 pp, Quality PB, 978-1-879045-30-9 **$16.99**

Recovery from Codependence: A Jewish Twelve Steps Guide to Healing Your Soul *By Rabbi Kerry M. Olitzky* 6 x 9, 160 pp, Quality PB, 978-1-879045-32-3 **$13.95**

Twelve Jewish Steps to Recovery, 2nd Edition: A Personal Guide to Turning from Alcoholism & Other Addictions—Drugs, Food, Gambling, Sex ...
By Rabbi Kerry M. Olitzky and Stuart A. Copans, MD; Preface by Abraham J. Twerski, MD
6 x 9, 160 pp, Quality PB, 978-1-58023-409-2 **$16.99**

Current Events/History

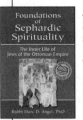

A Dream of Zion: American Jews Reflect on Why Israel Matters to Them
Edited by Rabbi Jeffrey K. Salkin Explores what Jewish people in America have to say
about Israel. 6 x 9, 304 pp, Quality PB, 978-1-58023-415-3 **$18.99**; HC, 978-1-58023-340-8 **$24.99**
Also Available: **A Dream of Zion Teacher's Guide** 8½ x 11, 32 pp, PB, 978-1-58023-356-9 **$8.99**

The Ethiopian Jews of Israel: Personal Stories of Life in the Promised
Land *By Len Lyons, PhD; Foreword by Alan Dershowitz; Photographs by Ilan Ossendryver*
Recounts, through photographs and words, stories of Ethiopian Jews.
10 x 10½, 240 pp, 100 full-color photos, HC, 978-1-58023-323-1 **$34.99**

Foundations of Sephardic Spirituality: The Inner Life of Jews of the Ottoman Empire
By Rabbi Marc D. Angel, PhD 6 x 9, 224 pp, Quality PB, 978-1-58023-341-5 **$18.99**

Hannah Senesh: Her Life and Diary, the First Complete Edition
By Hannah Senesh; Foreword by Marge Piercy; Preface by Eitan Senesh; Afterword by Roberta Grossman
6 x 9, 368 pp, b/w photos, Quality PB, 978-1-58023-342-2 **$19.99**

The Jewish Connection to Israel, the Promised Land: A Brief Introduction for
Christians *By Rabbi Eugene Korn, PhD* 5½ x 8½, 192 pp, Quality PB, 978-1-58023-318-7 **$14.99**

Judaism and Justice: The Jewish Passion to Repair the World
By Rabbi Sidney Schwarz 6 x 9, 352 pp, Quality PB, 978-1-58023-353-8 **$19.99**

The Story of the Jews: A 4,000-Year Adventure—A Graphic History Book
By Stan Mack 6 x 9, 288 pp, illus., Quality PB, 978-1-58023-155-8 **$16.99**

Ecology/Environment

A Wild Faith: Jewish Ways into Wilderness, Wilderness Ways into Judaism
By Rabbi Mike Comins; Foreword by Nigel Savage
Offers ways to enliven and deepen your spiritual life through wilderness experience.
6 x 9, 240 pp, Quality PB, 978-1-58023-316-3 **$16.99**

Ecology & the Jewish Spirit: Where Nature & the Sacred Meet
Edited by Ellen Bernstein 6 x 9, 288 pp, Quality PB, 978-1-58023-082-7 **$18.99**

Torah of the Earth: Exploring 4,000 Years of Ecology in Jewish Thought
Vol. 1: Biblical Israel & Rabbinic Judaism
Vol. 2: Zionism & Eco-Judaism
Edited by Rabbi Arthur Waskow Vol. 1: 6 x 9, 272 pp, Quality PB, 978-1-58023-086-5 **$19.95**
Vol. 2: 6 x 9, 336 pp, Quality PB, 978-1-58023-087-2 **$19.95**

The Way Into Judaism and the Environment *By Jeremy Benstein, PhD*
6 x 9, 288 pp, Quality PB, 978-1-58023-368-2 **$18.99**; HC, 978-1-58023-268-5 **$24.99**

Grief/Healing

Healing and the Jewish Imagination: Spiritual and Practical
Perspectives on Judaism and Health *Edited by Rabbi William Cutter, PhD*
Explores Judaism for comfort in times of illness and perspectives on suffering.
6 x 9, 240 pp, Quality PB, 978-1-58023-373-6 **$19.99**; HC, 978-1-58023-314-9 **$24.99**

Grief in Our Seasons: A Mourner's Kaddish Companion *By Rabbi Kerry M. Olitzky*
4½ x 6½, 448 pp, Quality PB, 978-1-879045-55-2 **$15.95**

Healing of Soul, Healing of Body: Spiritual Leaders Unfold the Strength & Solace
in Psalms *Edited by Rabbi Simkha Y. Weintraub, CSW*
6 x 9, 128 pp, 2-color illus. text, Quality PB, 978-1-879045-31-6 **$16.99**

Mourning & Mitzvah, 2nd Edition: A Guided Journal for Walking the Mourner's
Path through Grief to Healing *By Anne Brener, LCSW*
7½ x 9, 304 pp, Quality PB, 978-1-58023-113-8 **$19.99**

Tears of Sorrow, Seeds of Hope, 2nd Edition: A Jewish Spiritual Companion for
Infertility and Pregnancy Loss *By Rabbi Nina Beth Cardin*
6 x 9, 208 pp, Quality PB, 978-1-58023-233-3 **$18.99**

A Time to Mourn, a Time to Comfort, 2nd Edition: A Guide to Jewish
Bereavement *By Dr. Ron Wolfson; Preface by Rabbi David J. Wolpe*
7 x 9, 384 pp, Quality PB, 978-1-58023-253-1 **$19.99**

When a Grandparent Dies: A Kid's Own Remembering Workbook for Dealing
with Shiva and the Year Beyond *By Nechama Liss-Levinson, PhD*
8 x 10, 48 pp, 2-color text, HC, 978-1-879045-44-6 **$15.95** *For ages 7–13*

Inspiration

The Seven Questions You're Asked in Heaven: Reviewing and Renewing Your Life on Earth *By Dr. Ron Wolfson*
An intriguing and entertaining resource for living a life that matters.
6 x 9, 176 pp, Quality PB, 978-1-58023-407-8 **$16.99**

Happiness and the Human Spirit: The Spirituality of Becoming the Best You Can Be *By Abraham J. Twerski, MD*
Shows you that true happiness is attainable once you stop looking outside yourself for the source. 6 x 9, 176 pp, Quality PB, 978-1-58023-404-7 **$16.99**; HC, 978-1-58023-343-9 **$19.99**

Life's Daily Blessings: Inspiring Reflections on Gratitude and Joy for Every Day, Based on Jewish Wisdom *By Rabbi Kerry M. Olitzky* 4½ x 6½, 368 pp, Quality PB, 978-1-58023-396-5 **$16.99**

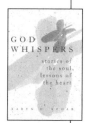

The Bridge to Forgiveness: Stories and Prayers for Finding God and Restoring Wholeness *By Rabbi Karyn D. Kedar*
Examines how forgiveness can be the bridge that connects us to wholeness and peace.
6 x 9, 176 pp, HC, 978-1-58023-324-8 **$19.99**

God's To-Do List: 103 Ways to Be an Angel and Do God's Work on Earth
By Dr. Ron Wolfson 6 x 9, 144 pp, Quality PB, 978-1-58023-301-9 **$16.99**

Our Dance with God: Finding Prayer, Perspective and Meaning in the Stories of Our Lives *By Karyn D. Kedar* 6 x 9, 176 pp, Quality PB, 978-1-58023-202-9 **$16.99**

Also Available: **The Dance of the Dolphin** (HC edition of Our Dance with God)
6 x 9, 176 pp, HC, 978-1-58023-154-1 **$19.95**

The Empty Chair: Finding Hope and Joy—Timeless Wisdom from a Hasidic Master, Rebbe Nachman of Breslov *Adapted by Moshe Mykoff and the Breslov Research Institute*
4 x 6, 128 pp, Deluxe PB w/ flaps, 978-1-879045-67-5 **$9.99**

The Gentle Weapon: Prayers for Everyday and Not-So-Everyday Moments— Timeless Wisdom from the Teachings of the Hasidic Master, Rebbe Nachman of Breslov *Adapted by Moshe Mykoff and S. C. Mizrahi, together with the Breslov Research Institute*
4 x 6, 144 pp, Deluxe PB w/ flaps, 978-1-58023-022-3 **$9.99**

God Whispers: Stories of the Soul, Lessons of the Heart *By Karyn D. Kedar*
6 x 9, 176 pp, Quality PB, 978-1-58023-088-9 **$15.95**

Restful Reflections: Nighttime Inspiration to Calm the Soul, Based on Jewish Wisdom *By Rabbi Kerry M. Olitzky and Rabbi Lori Forman* 4½ x 6½, 448 pp, Quality PB, 978-1-58023-091-9 **$15.95**

Sacred Intentions: Daily Inspiration to Strengthen the Spirit, Based on Jewish Wisdom *By Rabbi Kerry M. Olitzky and Rabbi Lori Forman* 4½ x 6½, 448 pp, Quality PB, 978-1-58023-061-2 **$15.95**

Kabbalah/Mysticism

Seek My Face: A Jewish Mystical Theology *By Arthur Green*
6 x 9, 304 pp, Quality PB, 978-1-58023-130-5 **$19.95**

Zohar: Annotated & Explained *Translated and annotated by Daniel C. Matt; Foreword by Andrew Harvey* 5½ x 8½, 176 pp, Quality PB, 978-1-893361-51-5 **$15.99**
(A book from SkyLight Paths, Jewish Lights' sister imprint)

Ehyeh: A Kabbalah for Tomorrow
By Arthur Green 6 x 9, 224 pp, Quality PB, 978-1-58023-213-5 **$16.99**

The Flame of the Heart: Prayers of a Chasidic Mystic
By Reb Noson of Breslov; Translated and adapted by David Sears, with the Breslov Research Institute
5 x 7¼, 160 pp, Quality PB, 978-1-58023-246-3 **$15.99**

The Gift of Kabbalah: Discovering the Secrets of Heaven, Renewing Your Life on Earth
By Tamar Frankiel, PhD 6 x 9, 256 pp, Quality PB, 978-1-58023-141-1 **$16.95**

Kabbalah: A Brief Introduction for Christians
By Tamar Frankiel, PhD 5½ x 8½, 208 pp, Quality PB, 978-1-58023-303-3 **$16.99**

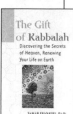

The Lost Princess & Other Kabbalistic Tales of Rebbe Nachman of Breslov
The Seven Beggars & Other Kabbalistic Tales of Rebbe Nachman of Breslov
Translated by Rabbi Aryeh Kaplan; Preface by Rabbi Chaim Kramer
Lost Princess: 6 x 9, 400 pp, Quality PB, 978-1-58023-217-3 **$18.99**
Seven Beggars: 6 x 9, 192 pp, Quality PB, 978-1-58023-250-0 **$16.99**

See also *The Way Into Jewish Mystical Tradition* in The Way Into... Series.

Holidays/Holy Days

Rosh Hashanah Readings: Inspiration, Information and Contemplation
Yom Kippur Readings: Inspiration, Information and Contemplation
Edited by Rabbi Dov Peretz Elkins; Section Introductions from Arthur Green's These Are the Words
An extraordinary collection of readings, prayers and insights that will enable you
to enter into the spirit of the High Holy Days in a personal and powerful way, per-
mitting the meaning of the Jewish New Year to enter the heart.
Rosh Hashanah: 6 x 9, 400 pp, HC, 978-1-58023-239-5 **$24.99**
Yom Kippur: 6 x 9, 368 pp, HC, 978-1-58023-271-5 **$24.99**

Jewish Holidays: A Brief Introduction for Christians
By Rabbi Kerry M. Olitzky and Rabbi Daniel Judson
5½ x 8½, 176 pp, Quality PB, 978-1-58023-302-6 **$16.99**

Reclaiming Judaism as a Spiritual Practice: Holy Days and Shabbat
By Rabbi Goldie Milgram
7 x 9, 272 pp, Quality PB, 978-1-58023-205-0 **$19.99**

7th Heaven: Celebrating Shabbat with Rebbe Nachman of Breslov
By Moshe Mykoff with the Breslov Research Institute
5⅛ x 8¼, 224 pp, Deluxe PB w/ flaps, 978-1-58023-175-6 **$18.95**

Shabbat, 2nd Edition: The Family Guide to Preparing for and Celebrating the Sabbath
By Dr. Ron Wolfson 7 x 9, 320 pp, illus., Quality PB, 978-1-58023-164-0 **$19.99**

Hanukkah, 2nd Edition: The Family Guide to Spiritual Celebration
By Dr. Ron Wolfson. Edited by Joel Lurie Grishaver.
7 x 9, 240 pp, illus., Quality PB, 978-1-58023-122-0 **$18.95**

The Jewish Family Fun Book, 2nd Edition: Holiday Projects, Everyday Activities,
and Travel Ideas with Jewish Themes *By Danielle Dardashti and Roni Sarig; Illus. by Avi Katz*
6 x 9, 304 pp, 70+ b/w illus. & diagrams, Quality PB, 978-1-58023-333-0 **$18.99**

The Jewish Lights Book of Fun Classroom Activities: Simple and Seasonal
Projects for Teachers and Students *By Danielle Dardashti and Roni Sarig*
6 x 9, 240 pp, Quality PB, 978-1-58023-206-7 **$19.99**

Passover

My People's Passover Haggadah
Traditional Texts, Modern Commentaries
Edited by Rabbi Lawrence A. Hoffman, PhD, and David Arnow, PhD
A diverse and exciting collection of commentaries on the traditional Passover
Haggadah—in two volumes!
Vol. 1: 7 x 10, 304 pp, HC, 978-1-58023-354-5 **$24.99**
Vol. 2: 7 x 10, 320 pp, HC, 978-1-58023-346-0 **$24.99**

Leading the Passover Journey
The Seder's Meaning Revealed, the Haggadah's Story Retold
By Rabbi Nathan Laufer
Uncovers the hidden meaning of the Seder's rituals and customs.
6 x 9, 224 pp, Quality PB, 978-1-58023-399-6 **$18.99**; HC, 978-1-58023-211-1 **$24.99**

The Women's Passover Companion: Women's Reflections on the Festival of Freedom
Edited by Rabbi Sharon Cohen Anisfeld, Tara Mohr and Catherine Spector; Foreword by Paula E. Hyman
6 x 9, 352 pp, Quality PB, 978-1-58023-231-9 **$19.99**

The Women's Seder Sourcebook: Rituals & Readings for Use at the Passover Seder
Edited by Rabbi Sharon Cohen Anisfeld, Tara Mohr and Catherine Spector; Foreword by Paula E. Hyman
6 x 9, 384 pp, Quality PB, 978-1-58023-232-6 **$19.99**

Creating Lively Passover Seders: A Sourcebook of Engaging Tales, Texts & Activities
By David Arnow, PhD 7 x 9, 416 pp, Quality PB, 978-1-58023-184-8 **$24.99**

Passover, 2nd Edition: The Family Guide to Spiritual Celebration
By Dr. Ron Wolfson with Joel Lurie Grishaver 7 x 9, 352 pp, Quality PB, 978-1-58023-174-9 **$19.95**

Life Cycle
Marriage/Parenting/Family/Aging

The New Jewish Baby Album: Creating and Celebrating the Beginning of a Spiritual Life—A Jewish Lights Companion
By the Editors at Jewish Lights; Foreword by Anita Diamant; Preface by Rabbi Sandy Eisenberg Sasso
A spiritual keepsake that will be treasured for generations. More than just a memory book, *shows you how—and why it's important*—to create a Jewish home and a Jewish life. 8 x 10, 64 pp, Deluxe Padded HC, Full-color illus., 978-1-58023-138-1 **$19.95**

The Jewish Pregnancy Book: A Resource for the Soul, Body & Mind during Pregnancy, Birth & the First Three Months
By Sandy Falk, MD, and Rabbi Daniel Judson, with Steven A. Rapp
Includes medical information, prayers and rituals for each stage of pregnancy, from a liberal Jewish perspective. 7 x 10, 208 pp, b/w photos, Quality PB, 978-1-58023-178-7 **$16.95**

Celebrating Your New Jewish Daughter: Creating Jewish Ways to Welcome Baby Girls into the Covenant—New and Traditional Ceremonies *By Debra Nussbaum Cohen; Foreword by Rabbi Sandy Eisenberg Sasso* 6 x 9, 272 pp, Quality PB, 978-1-58023-090-2 **$18.95**

The New Jewish Baby Book, 2nd Edition: Names, Ceremonies & Customs—A Guide for Today's Families *By Anita Diamant* 6 x 9, 336 pp, Quality PB, 978-1-58023-251-7 **$19.99**

Parenting as a Spiritual Journey: Deepening Ordinary and Extraordinary Events into Sacred Occasions *By Rabbi Nancy Fuchs-Kreimer*
6 x 9, 224 pp, Quality PB, 978-1-58023-016-2 **$16.95**

Parenting Jewish Teens: A Guide for the Perplexed
By Joanne Doades
Explores the questions and issues that shape the world in which today's Jewish teenagers live and offers constructive advice to parents.
6 x 9, 176 pp, Quality PB, 978-1-58023-305-7 **$16.99**

Judaism for Two: A Spiritual Guide for Strengthening and Celebrating Your Loving Relationship *By Rabbi Nancy Fuchs-Kreimer, PhD, and Rabbi Nancy H. Wiener, DMin; Foreword by Rabbi Elliot N. Dorff*
Addresses the ways Jewish teachings can enhance and strengthen committed relationships. 6 x 9, 224 pp, Quality PB, 978-1-58023-254-8 **$16.99**

The Creative Jewish Wedding Book, 2nd Edition: A Hands-On Guide to New & Old Traditions, Ceremonies & Celebrations *By Gabrielle Kaplan-Mayer*
9 x 9, 288 pp, b/w photos, Quality PB, 978-1-58023-398-9 **$19.99**

Divorce Is a Mitzvah: A Practical Guide to Finding Wholeness and Holiness When Your Marriage Dies *By Rabbi Perry Netter; Afterword by Rabbi Laura Geller*
6 x 9, 224 pp, Quality PB, 978-1-58023-172-5 **$16.95**

Embracing the Covenant: Converts to Judaism Talk About Why & How
By Rabbi Allan Berkowitz and Patti Moskovitz 6 x 9, 192 pp, Quality PB, 978-1-879045-50-7 **$16.95**

The Guide to Jewish Interfaith Family Life: An InterfaithFamily.com Handbook *Edited by Ronnie Friedland and Edmund Case*
6 x 9, 384 pp, Quality PB, 978-1-58023-153-4 **$18.95**

A Heart of Wisdom: Making the Jewish Journey from Midlife through the Elder Years *Edited by Susan Berrin; Foreword by Harold Kushner*
6 x 9, 384 pp, Quality PB, 978-1-58023-051-3 **$18.95**

Introducing My Faith and My Community
The Jewish Outreach Institute Guide for the Christian in a Jewish Interfaith Relationship
By Rabbi Kerry M. Olitzky 6 x 9, 176 pp, Quality PB, 978-1-58023-192-3 **$16.99**

Making a Successful Jewish Interfaith Marriage: The Jewish Outreach Institute Guide to Opportunities, Challenges and Resources *By Rabbi Kerry M. Olitzky with Joan Peterson Littman*
6 x 9, 176 pp, Quality PB, 978-1-58023-170-1 **$16.95**

So That Your Values Live On: Ethical Wills and How to Prepare Them
Edited by Jack Riemer and Nathaniel Stampfer
6 x 9, 272 pp, Quality PB, 978-1-879045-34-7 **$18.99**

Spirituality

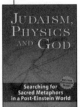

Journeys to a Jewish Life: Inspiring Stories from the Spiritual Journeys of American Jews *By Paula Amann*
Examines the soul treks of Jews lost and found. 6 x 9, 208 pp, HC, 978-1-58023-317-0 **$19.99**

The Adventures of Rabbi Harvey: A Graphic Novel of Jewish Wisdom and Wit in the Wild West *By Steve Sheinkin*
Jewish and American folktales combine in this witty and original graphic novel collection. Creatively retold and set on the western frontier of the 1870s.
6 x 9, 144 pp, Full-color illus., Quality PB, 978-1-58023-310-1 **$16.99**

Rabbi Harvey Rides Again: A Graphic Novel of Jewish Folktales Let Loose in the Wild West *By Steve Sheinkin* 6 x 9, 144 pp, Full-color illus., Quality PB, 978-1-58023-347-7 **$16.99**

Ethics of the Sages: *Pirke Avot*—Annotated & Explained
Translation & Annotation by Rabbi Rami Shapiro 5½ x 8½, 192 pp, Quality PB, 978-1-59473-207-2
$16.99 *(A book from SkyLight Paths, Jewish Lights' sister imprint)*

A Book of Life: Embracing Judaism as a Spiritual Practice
By Rabbi Michael Strassfeld 6 x 9, 544 pp, Quality PB, 978-1-58023-247-0 **$19.99**

Meaning and Mitzvah: Daily Practices for Reclaiming Judaism through Prayer, God, Torah, Hebrew, Mitzvot and Peoplehood *By Rabbi Goldie Milgram*
7 x 9, 336 pp, Quality PB, 978-1-58023-256-2 **$19.99**

The Soul of the Story: Meetings with Remarkable People
By Rabbi David Zeller 6 x 9, 288 pp, HC, 978-1-58023-272-2 **$21.99**

Aleph-Bet Yoga: Embodying the Hebrew Letters for Physical and Spiritual Well-Being
By Steven A. Rapp; Foreword by Tamar Frankiel, PhD, and Judy Greenfeld; Preface by Hart Lazer
7 x 10, 128 pp, b/w photos, Quality PB, Layflat binding, 978-1-58023-162-6 **$16.95**

Does the Soul Survive? A Jewish Journey to Belief in Afterlife, Past Lives & Living with Purpose *By Rabbi Elie Kaplan Spitz; Foreword by Brian L. Weiss, MD*
6 x 9, 288 pp, Quality PB, 978-1-58023-165-7 **$16.99**

First Steps to a New Jewish Spirit: Reb Zalman's Guide to Recapturing the Intimacy & Ecstasy in Your Relationship with God *By Rabbi Zalman M. Schachter-Shalomi with Donald Gropman* 6 x 9, 144 pp, Quality PB, 978-1-58023-182-4 **$16.95**

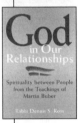

God in Our Relationships: Spirituality between People from the Teachings of Martin Buber *By Rabbi Dennis S. Ross* 5½ x 8½, 160 pp, Quality PB, 978-1-58023-147-3 **$16.95**

Judaism, Physics and God: Searching for Sacred Metaphors in a Post-Einstein World
By Rabbi David W. Nelson 6 x 9, 352 pp, Quality PB, inc. reader's discussion guide,
978-1-58023-306-4 **$18.99**; HC, 352 pp, 978-1-58023-252-4 **$24.99**

The Jewish Lights Spirituality Handbook: A Guide to Understanding, Exploring & Living a Spiritual Life *Edited by Stuart M. Matlins*
What exactly is "Jewish" about spirituality? How do I make it a part of my life? Fifty of today's foremost spiritual leaders share their ideas and experience with us.
6 x 9, 456 pp, Quality PB, 978-1-58023-093-3 **$19.99**

Bringing the Psalms to Life: How to Understand and Use the Book of Psalms
By Rabbi Daniel F. Polish, PhD 6 x 9, 208 pp, Quality PB, 978-1-58023-157-2 **$16.95**

God & the Big Bang: Discovering Harmony between Science & Spirituality
By Dr. Daniel C. Matt 6 x 9, 216 pp, Quality PB, 978-1-879045-89-7 **$16.99**

Minding the Temple of the Soul: Balancing Body, Mind, and Spirit through Traditional Jewish Prayer, Movement, and Meditation *By Tamar Frankiel, PhD, and Judy Greenfeld*
7 x 10, 184 pp, illus., Quality PB, 978-1-879045-64-4 **$16.95**

One God Clapping: The Spiritual Path of a Zen Rabbi *By Alan Lew with Sherril Jaffe*
5½ x 8½, 336 pp, Quality PB, 978-1-58023-115-2 **$16.95**

There Is No Messiah ... and You're It: The Stunning Transformation of Judaism's Most Provocative Idea *By Rabbi Robert N. Levine, DD*
6 x 9, 192 pp, Quality PB, 978-1-58023-255-5 **$16.99**

These Are the Words: A Vocabulary of Jewish Spiritual Life
By Rabbi Arthur Green, PhD 6 x 9, 304 pp, Quality PB, 978-1-58023-107-7 **$18.95**

Spirituality/Lawrence Kushner

The Book of Letters: A Mystical Hebrew Alphabet
Popular HC Edition, 6 x 9, 80 pp, 2-color text, 978-1-879045-00-2 **$24.95**
Collector's Limited Edition, 9 x 12, 80 pp, gold-foil-embossed pages, w/ limited-edition silkscreened
print, 978-1-879045-04-0 **$349.00**

The Book of Miracles: A Young Person's Guide to Jewish Spiritual Awareness
6 x 9, 96 pp, 2-color illus., HC, 978-1-879045-78-1 **$16.95** *For ages 9–13*

The Book of Words: Talking Spiritual Life, Living Spiritual Talk
6 x 9, 160 pp, Quality PB, 978-1-58023-020-9 **$16.95**

Eyes Remade for Wonder: A Lawrence Kushner Reader   *Introduction by Thomas Moore*
6 x 9, 240 pp, Quality PB, 978-1-58023-042-1 **$18.95**

Filling Words with Light: Hasidic and Mystical Reflections on Jewish Prayer
By Rabbi Lawrence Kushner and Rabbi Nehemia Polen
5½ x 8½, 176 pp, Quality PB, 978-1-58023-238-8 **$16.99**; HC, 978-1-58023-216-6 **$21.99**

God Was in This Place & I, i Did Not Know: Finding Self, Spirituality and
Ultimate Meaning   6 x 9, 192 pp, Quality PB, 978-1-879045-33-0 **$16.95**

Honey from the Rock: An Introduction to Jewish Mysticism
6 x 9, 176 pp, Quality PB, 978-1-58023-073-5 **$16.95**

Invisible Lines of Connection: Sacred Stories of the Ordinary
5½ x 8½, 160 pp, Quality PB, 978-1-879045-98-9 **$15.95**

Jewish Spirituality: A Brief Introduction for Christians
5½ x 8½, 112 pp, Quality PB, 978-1-58023-150-3 **$12.95**

The River of Light: Jewish Mystical Awareness
6 x 9, 192 pp, Quality PB, 978-1-58023-096-4 **$16.95**

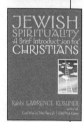

The Way Into Jewish Mystical Tradition
6 x 9, 224 pp, Quality PB, 978-1-58023-200-5 **$18.99**; HC, 978-1-58023-029-2 **$21.95**

Spirituality/Prayer

My People's Passover Haggadah: Traditional Texts, Modern Commentaries
Edited by Rabbi Lawrence A. Hoffman, PhD, and David Arnow, PhD   Diverse commentaries
on the traditional Passover Haggadah—in two volumes! Vol. 1: 7 x 10, 304 pp, HC
978-1-58023-354-5 **$24.99**; Vol. 2: 7 x 10, 320 pp, HC, 978-1-58023-346-0 **$24.99**

Witnesses to the One: The Spiritual History of the *Sh'ma* *By Rabbi Joseph B. Meszler;*
Foreword by Rabbi Elyse Goldstein 6 x 9, 176 pp, Quality PB, 978-1-58023-400-9 **$16.99**; HC,
978-1-58023-309-5 **$19.99**

My People's Prayer Book Series

Traditional Prayers, Modern Commentaries   *Edited by Rabbi Lawrence A. Hoffman, PhD*
Provides diverse and exciting commentary to the traditional liturgy. Will help you
find new wisdom in Jewish prayer, and bring liturgy into your life. Each book
includes Hebrew text, modern translation and commentaries from all perspectives
of the Jewish world.

Vol. 1—The *Sh'ma* and Its Blessings
   7 x 10, 168 pp, HC, 978-1-879045-79-8 **$24.99**

Vol. 2—The *Amidah*   7 x 10, 240 pp, HC, 978-1-879045-80-4 **$24.95**

Vol. 3—*P'sukei D'zimrah* (Morning Psalms)
   7 x 10, 240 pp, HC, 978-1-879045-81-1 **$24.95**

Vol. 4—*Seder K'riat Hatorah* (The Torah Service)
   7 x 10, 264 pp, HC, 978-1-879045-82-8 **$23.95**

Vol. 5—*Birkhot Hashachar* (Morning Blessings)
   7 x 10, 240 pp, HC, 978-1-879045-83-5 **$24.95**

Vol. 6—*Tachanun* and Concluding Prayers
   7 x 10, 240 pp, HC, 978-1-879045-84-2 **$24.95**

Vol. 7—Shabbat at Home   7 x 10, 240 pp, HC, 978-1-879045-85-9 **$24.95**

Vol. 8—*Kabbalat Shabbat* (Welcoming Shabbat in the Synagogue)
   7 x 10, 240 pp, HC, 978-1-58023-121-3 **$24.99**

Vol. 9—Welcoming the Night: *Minchah* and *Ma'ariv* (Afternoon and
   Evening Prayer) 7 x 10, 272 pp, HC, 978-1-58023-262-3 **$24.99**

Vol. 10—Shabbat Morning: *Shacharit* and *Musaf* (Morning and
   Additional Services) 7 x 10, 240 pp, HC, 978-1-58023-240-1 **$24.99**

Theology/Philosophy/The Way Into... Series

The Way Into... series offers an accessible and highly usable "guided tour" of the Jewish faith, people, history and beliefs—in total, an introduction to Judaism that will enable you to understand and interact with the sacred texts of the Jewish tradition. Each volume is written by a leading contemporary scholar and teacher, and explores one key aspect of Judaism. The Way Into... series enables all readers to achieve a real sense of Jewish cultural literacy through guided study.

The Way Into Encountering God in Judaism
By Rabbi Neil Gillman, PhD
For everyone who wants to understand how Jews have encountered God throughout history and today.
6 x 9, 240 pp, Quality PB, 978-1-58023-199-2 **$18.99**; HC, 978-1-58023-025-4 **$21.95**
Also Available: **The Jewish Approach to God:** A Brief Introduction for Christians
By Rabbi Neil Gillman, PhD
5½ x 8¼, 192 pp, Quality PB, 978-1-58023-190-9 **$16.95**

The Way Into Jewish Mystical Tradition
By Rabbi Lawrence Kushner
Allows readers to interact directly with the sacred mystical texts of the Jewish tradition. An accessible introduction to the concepts of Jewish mysticism, their religious and spiritual significance, and how they relate to life today.
6 x 9, 224 pp, Quality PB, 978-1-58023-200-5 **$18.99**; HC, 978-1-58023-029-2 **$21.95**

The Way Into Jewish Prayer
By Rabbi Lawrence A. Hoffman, PhD
Opens the door to 3,000 years of Jewish prayer, making available all anyone needs to feel at home in the Jewish way of communicating with God.
6 x 9, 208 pp, Quality PB, 978-1-58023-201-2 **$18.99**

Also Available: **The Way Into Jewish Prayer Teacher's Guide**
By Rabbi Jennifer Ossakow Goldsmith
8½ x 11, 42 pp, PB, 978-1-58023-345-3 **$8.99**
Download a free copy at www.jewishlights.com.

The Way Into Judaism and the Environment
By Jeremy Benstein, PhD
Explores the ways in which Judaism contributes to contemporary social-environmental issues, the extent to which Judaism is part of the problem and how it can be part of the solution.
6 x 9, 288 pp, Quality PB, 978-1-58023-368-2 **$18.99**; HC, 978-1-58023-268-5 **$24.99**

The Way Into Tikkun Olam (Repairing the World)
By Rabbi Elliot N. Dorff, PhD
An accessible introduction to the Jewish concept of the individual's responsibility to care for others and repair the world.
6 x 9, 304 pp, Quality PB, 978-1-58023-328-6 **$18.99**; 320 pp, HC, 978-1-58023-269-2 **$24.99**

The Way Into Torah
By Rabbi Norman J. Cohen, PhD
Helps guide in the exploration of the origins and development of Torah, explains why it should be studied and how to do it.
6 x 9, 176 pp, Quality PB, 978-1-58023-198-5 **$16.99**

The Way Into the Varieties of Jewishness
By Sylvia Barack Fishman, PhD
Explores the religious and historical understanding of what it has meant to be Jewish from ancient times to the present controversy over "Who is a Jew?"
6 x 9, 288 pp, Quality PB, 978-1-58023-367-5 **$18.99**; HC, 978-1-58023-030-8 **$24.99**

Theology/Philosophy

A Touch of the Sacred: A Theologian's Informal Guide to Jewish Belief
By Dr. Eugene B. Borowitz and Frances W. Schwartz
Explores the musings from the leading theologian of liberal Judaism.
6 x 9, 256 pp, Quality PB, 978-1-58023-416-0 **$16.99**; HC, 978-1-58023-337-8 **$21.99**

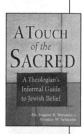

Talking about God: Exploring the Meaning of Religious Life with
Kierkegaard, Buber, Tillich and Heschel *By Daniel F. Polish, PhD*
Examines the meaning of the human religious experience with the greatest theologians of modern times. 6 x 9, 160 pp, Quality PB, 978-1-59473-272-0 **$16.99**
HC, 978-1-59473-230-0 **$21.99** *(A book from SkyLight Paths, Jewish Lights' sister imprint)*

Jews and Judaism in the 21st Century: Human Responsibility, the
Presence of God, and the Future of the Covenant *Edited by Rabbi Edward Feinstein;
Foreword by Paula E. Hyman* Five celebrated leaders in Judaism examine contemporary
Jewish life. 6 x 9, 192 pp, Quality PB, 978-1-58023-374-3 **$19.99**; HC, 978-1-58023-315-6 **$24.99**

Christians and Jews in Dialogue: Learning in the Presence of the Other
By Mary C. Boys and Sara S. Lee 6 x 9, 240 pp, Quality PB, 978-1-59473-254-6 **$18.99**
(A book from SkyLight Paths, Jewish Lights' sister imprint)

The Death of Death: Resurrection and Immortality in Jewish Thought
By Rabbi Neil Gillman, PhD 6 x 9, 336 pp, Quality PB, 978-1-58023-081-0 **$18.95**

Ethics of the Sages: *Pirke Avot*—Annotated & Explained
Translation & Annotation by Rabbi Rami Shapiro
5½ x 8½, 192 pp, Quality PB, 978-1-59473-207-2 **$16.99** *(A book from SkyLight Paths, Jewish Lights' sister imprint)*

Hasidic Tales: Annotated & Explained *Translation & Annotation by Rabbi Rami Shapiro*
5½ x 8½, 240 pp, Quality PB, 978-1-893361-86-7 **$16.95** *(A book from SkyLight Paths, Jewish Lights' sister imprint)*

A Heart of Many Rooms: Celebrating the Many Voices within Judaism
By Dr. David Hartman 6 x 9, 352 pp, Quality PB, 978-1-58023-156-5 **$19.95**

The Hebrew Prophets: Selections Annotated & Explained
Translation & Annotation by Rabbi Rami Shapiro; Foreword by Rabbi Zalman M. Schachter-Shalomi
5½ x 8½, 224 pp, Quality PB, 978-1-59473-037-5 **$16.99** *(A book from SkyLight Paths, Jewish Lights' sister imprint)*

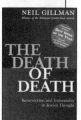

A Jewish Understanding of the New Testament
By Rabbi Samuel Sandmel; Preface by Rabbi David Sandmel
5½ x 8½, 368 pp, Quality PB, 978-1-59473-048-1 **$19.99** *(A book from SkyLight Paths, Jewish Lights' sister imprint)*

Keeping Faith with the Psalms: Deepen Your Relationship with God Using the Book
of Psalms *By Rabbi Daniel F. Polish, PhD* 6 x 9, 320 pp, Quality PB, 978-1-58023-300-2 **$18.99**

A Living Covenant: The Innovative Spirit in Traditional Judaism
By Dr. David Hartman 6 x 9, 368 pp, Quality PB, 978-1-58023-011-7 **$20.00**

Love and Terror in the God Encounter: The Theological Legacy of Rabbi Joseph
B. Soloveitchik *By Dr. David Hartman* 6 x 9, 240 pp, Quality PB, 978-1-58023-176-3 **$19.95**

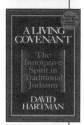

The Personhood of God: Biblical Theology, Human Faith and the Divine Image
By Dr. Yochanan Muffs; Foreword by Dr. David Hartman
6 x 9, 240 pp, Quality PB, 978-1-58023-338-5 **$18.99**; HC, 978-1-58023-265-4 **$24.99**

Traces of God: Seeing God in Torah, History and Everyday Life *By Rabbi Neil Gillman, PhD*
6 x 9, 240 pp, Quality PB, 978-1-58023-369-9 **$16.99**; HC, 978-1-58023-249-4 **$21.99**

We Jews and Jesus: Exploring Theological Differences for Mutual Understanding
By Rabbi Samuel Sandmel; Preface by Rabbi David Sandmel
6 x 9, 192 pp, Quality PB, 978-1-59473-208-9 **$16.99** *(A book from SkyLight Paths, Jewish Lights' sister imprint)*

Your Word Is Fire: The Hasidic Masters on Contemplative Prayer
Edited and translated by Rabbi Arthur Green, PhD, and Barry W. Holtz
6 x 9, 160 pp, Quality PB, 978-1-879045-25-5 **$15.95**

I Am Jewish
Personal Reflections Inspired by the Last Words of Daniel Pearl
Almost 150 Jews—both famous and not—from all walks of life, from all around
the world, write about many aspects of their Judaism.
Edited by Judea and Ruth Pearl 6 x 9, 304 pp, Deluxe PB w/ flaps, 978-1-58023-259-3 **$18.99**
Download a free copy of the *I Am Jewish Teacher's Guide* at www.jewishlights.com.

About Jewish Lights

People of all faiths and backgrounds yearn for books that attract, engage, educate, and spiritually inspire.

Our principal goal is to stimulate thought and help all people learn about who the Jewish People are, where they come from, and what the future can be made to hold. While people of our diverse Jewish heritage are the primary audience, our books speak to people in the Christian world as well and will broaden their understanding of Judaism and the roots of their own faith.

We bring to you authors who are at the forefront of spiritual thought and experience. While each has something different to say, they all say it in a voice that you can hear.

Our books are designed to welcome you and then to engage, stimulate, and inspire. We judge our success not only by whether or not our books are beautiful and commercially successful, but by whether or not they make a difference in your life.

For your information and convenience, at the back of this book we have provided a list of other Jewish Lights books you might find interesting and useful. They cover all the categories of your life:

Bar/Bat Mitzvah
Bible Study / Midrash
Children's Books
Congregation Resources
Current Events / History
Ecology / Environment
Fiction: Mystery, Science Fiction
Grief / Healing
Holidays / Holy Days
Inspiration
Kabbalah / Mysticism / Enneagram

Life Cycle
Meditation
Men's Interest
Parenting
Prayer / Ritual / Sacred Practice
Social Justice
Spirituality
Theology / Philosophy
Travel
12-Step
Women's Interest

Stuart M. Matlins, Publisher

Or phone, fax, mail or e-mail to: **JEWISH LIGHTS Publishing**
Sunset Farm Offices, Route 4 • P.O. Box 237 • Woodstock, Vermont 05091
Tel: (802) 457-4000 • Fax: (802) 457-4004 • www.jewishlights.com
Credit card orders: (800) 962-4544 (8:30AM–5:30PM ET Monday–Friday)
Generous discounts on quantity orders. SATISFACTION GUARANTEED. Prices subject to change.

For more information about each book, visit our website at www.jewishlights.com